W9-BTR-545

JERSEY DINERS

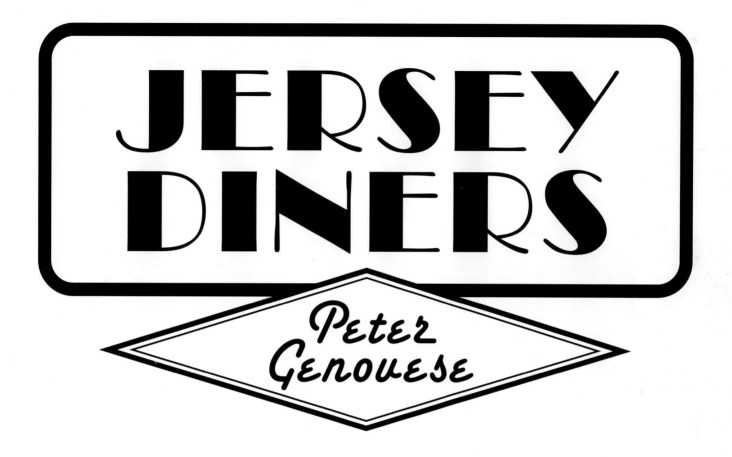

Peter Genovese

Rivergate Books

An Imprint of Rutgers University Press
New Brunswick, New Jersey

Route 46 East at Route 93, Ridgefield.

Frontispiece: Walt's Drive-In, on Route 46 in Caldwell, had a B-29 tail assembly sticking out of the roof. It came from a plane that had crashed at a nearby airport. (Courtesy of University of Louisville Photographic Archives)

First paperback printing, 2006

Library of Congress Cataloging-in-Publication Data

Genovese, Peter, 1952—
    Jersey diners / Peter Genovese.
      p. cm.
    ISBN 0-8135-2350-8 (cloth : alk. paper)
    ISBN 0-8135-3876-9 (pbk : alk. paper)
    1. Diners (Restaurants)—New Jersey.   I. Title.
TX945.G39   1996
647.95749—dc20
                            96-18137
                            CIP

British Cataloging-in-Publication information available

Copyright © 1996 by Peter Genovese
All rights reserved.
No part of this book may be reproduced or utilized in any form or by any means, electronic or mechanical, or by any information storage and retrieval system, without written permission from the publisher. Please contact Rutgers University Press, Livingston Campus, Bldg. 4161, P.O. Box 5062, New Brunswick, New Jersey 08903. The only exception to this prohibition is "fair use" as defined by U.S. copyright law.

Design by John Romer

Manufactured in China

To Jessica,
with the five-star smile,

◆ ◆ ◆  ◆ ◆ ◆

and all the happy waitresses out there

Sign for the former Horseshoe Diner,
Boyle Plaza, Jersey City.

Miss America Diner, Jersey City.

CONTENTS

Don's Diner, Irvington.

Summit Diner, 5:30 A.M. The lights inside usually flicker several times, as if the diner itself is not quite awake.

OPENING TIME

Early morning, pitch black out. The center of town deserted. The train station empty.

At one street corner, a glimmer of light. A building, its windows aglow. Squat, odd-looking, like a railroad car.

Noise from inside. Conversation, spoons tinkling, plates clattering, a sizzling, crackling sound.

5:30 A.M. The Summit Diner is open for business.

"Thirty years I've come to this joint," says Patrolman James Pantini, settling into a booth. He laughs. "Probably caused my heart attack. How many sliders I've had out of this place."

A slider—Taylor ham, egg, and cheese on a roll—is on the grill, but it's not for him.

Three guys, each wearing orange shirts and green pants, are hunched over the counter, one with a plate of eggs, another with a slider, the third with a cup of coffee.

Two more guys wearing the same uniform walk in.

Public works crew, city of Summit.

"Hemingway ate here," declares Carmine D'Annunzio. He looks over at cook and co-owner Jimmy Greberis. "What seat did he sit at?"

Jimmy shrugs, the gesture saying, Don't ask me these questions so early in the morning.

The lights flicker several times, as if the diner itself is not quite awake.

Limousine driver Barry Amatucci begins the day with eggs and hash browns at the Summit Diner.

John Greberis cooks up that breakfast favorite: pork-roll-and-egg sandwiches.

"Good morning!" a woman says cheerily as she enters.

"Good morning!" replies a chorus of men at the counter.

"What the hell is this stuff?" grumbles Calvin Stone. He looks at the syrup packet for his pancakes. "What the hell contents is this?"

The bald-headed Stone, a member of the Summit police department meter patrol, checks his watch, then takes a gulp from his big glass of milk.

"I got to go," he announces, getting up.

"Bathroom's right over there," Saul Valencia, a mechanic, says helpfully.

"Hey, Cal," Valencia says as Stone walks to the door. "Don't get run over."

At one end of the diner are a gas station owner and a garbageman; at the other, two men in business suits.

Tom Hoesly, who works at a nearby Getty station, is eating bacon and eggs. Grapefruit juice, no coffee.

"Drink too much," he says. "Have ten cups before ten. Couple when I get up, couple on the way over. And I'll bring five with me out of here."

Styrofoam cups are lined up on the counter for take-out customers.

Mel Acuna, the cook, tosses three pieces of bacon on the grill.

Outside, the sun is up. The air is crisp and clear, the sky blue.

"In here, you get a man-sized meatloaf," Pantini says. "A moose couldn't finish one of those."

Later John Anastos will sit in a booth and smile. He owns the Summit Diner with Jimmy Greberis. Bill Nicholas, co-owner of the Harris Diner, is John's father's cousin. Both Nicholas and his partner, Bill Marmaras, are Jimmy Greberis's uncles.

"It gets very confusing," Anastos says.

He looks around the 1929 diner, which, legend has it, Hemingway often visited.

Summit Diner.

Summit Diner, 6:15 A.M. Hemingway, local legend has it, ate here several times.

Everyone from truck drivers to corporate "suits" can be found at the Summit first thing in the morning.

Behind Anastos, a waitress bobs in and out of the booths; a customer walks over to the diner's self-service water dispenser. The conversation, all around, is lively.

"I call it 'the Show,'" Anastos says. "I say, you sit up at the counter, you're going to have to pay for what's going on."

This book is the result of scores of interviews with diner owners, employees, and customers; and of hundreds of hours of early mornings, midafternoons, and late nights in diners throughout New Jersey.

It is not a diner reference book; there will be no chapters on the evolution of napkin dispensers or the development of tufted Naugahyde. There are several chapters on diner history, but most of the history here is wound through the other chapters, in the profiles of diners and diner people.

There will be no quotes from scholars, none of the rarefied language used whenever so-called experts start talking about diners. "The mood in the diner," proclaimed a story in one well-known newspaper, "is one of boisterous egalitarianism."

I guarantee that "boisterous egalitarianism" is one phrase you will never hear in a diner.

What the writer was trying to say: A diner is not only a place to eat, it is a hangout, a community center, often more of a town hall than Town Hall is. Wealth, possessions, background count for little; inside, everyone is equal.

What is a diner? Purists say it must be a structure that is made in the factory and trucked to its site. The diners listed in the directory include a handful of restaurants with "diner" in their name that are not prefab structures. The Garden State Diner at Newark International Airport does not meet the purists' definition, but it is as surely a diner as any classic one. Why get hung up on technicalities? It's the atmosphere that counts. "What's a diner?" A diner owner told the radio station New Jersey 101.5, "You walk in, you can get anything you want at any time you want."

You won't find any cutesy dinerspeak here, none of that "Adam and Eve on a log" stuff that some writers seem to think all diner employees use. In New Jersey, at least, they don't talk that way.

Diners weren't born here, but there are more diners in New Jersey than in any other state. It's amazing how little we know about diners considering how much they are a part of our everyday life. One county historical preservation officer puts the number of New Jersey diners at 850, while a major daily newspaper confidently states that there are "fewer than 200." Both are uneducated guesses. There are 570 diners in the state, at last count. How do I know? I went through every phone book in the state, talked to people in the know, and came up with 570. I've stopped, though not necessarily eaten, at every one.

Why are there so many diners in New Jersey? One reason is that many of the diner companies traditionally were located here; few diners made it beyond the East Coast because of the prohibitive cost of trucking them thousands of miles. Today three of the four remaining diner manufacturers are located in New Jersey.

Pete Horn, one of the dozen or so Summit Department of Public Works garbagemen who can be found in the diner shortly after it opens.

But something else is at work as well. New Jersey is the most highway-intensive state. Millions of people drive in and through the Garden State every day; they've got to eat somewhere. No one in New Jersey lives far from a diner; they are in fully half of the state's 567 municipalities.

I also like to think there's something innately New Jersey about a diner. Diners are colorful and kitschy, and in New Jersey, which Rutgers University professor Michael Aaron Rockland calls the roadside pop architecture capital of the world, they have found a home.

If New Jersey has one redeeming social value, it's the diner.

This book will be a kind of diner documentary, slices of life along the endless diner highway. The road may go on forever, but in New Jersey there's always a diner on the way.

So settle back with a cup of coffee, maybe a slice of apple pie. Like some ice cream on that?

Welcome to the world of Jersey diners. Welcome to "the Show."

A FIVE-STAR DINER

It sits up on a hill, all red and shiny, surrounded by a sky so blue that it nearly hurts your eyes. Flowers sparkle in the bright midafternoon sun; an American flag flutters in the breeze.

There may be no more perfect setting for a diner in New Jersey.

Inside, the sun streams through the yellow curtains, suffusing everything—the soft yellow walls, light green booths, the stainless steel—with a golden glow.

Perfect spot for a nice country breakfast, maybe some eggs, bacon, and home fries—the diner is known for its home fries—or waffles with fresh strawberries or blueberries.

Like soup? You've come to the right place.

The Five Star Diner on Route 206 in Branchville wasn't always a five-star place.

"The previous owners didn't take very good care of it," Jerry Heater says. "We had to put new drains in. The timbers were all rotted; we went in there, replaced them.

"We rebuilt practically the whole place," he adds. "Put in new equipment, new hood and exhaust system, two new grills, two new refrigerators, new freezer."

He smiles. "We're not done yet."

Anybody who thinks that when you buy a diner you just open the door and wait for customers should talk to the Heaters. They've owned the Five Star for thirteen years. It was Linda Heater's idea. A former clerical worker, she got tired of sitting all day at work. She asked a friend in real estate, "Find me something." Her friend said, "How about a diner?"

The diner was originally called J.D.'s, then the Five Star, apparently because the owner had five kids.

Five Star Diner, Branchville.

Her day almost over, waitress Jessica Hemmerlin cleans off the stools at the Five Star Diner.

"She wanted to be busy, more active," her husband says. "She is. She's working seven days a week."

The Silk City diner was originally elsewhere—Jerry heard Riverdale, in Morris County—before J. D. Reed bought the diner and moved it to Sussex County. The diner was called J.D.'s, then the Five Star, apparently because the previous owners had five kids.

"We came here cold," says Jerry, superintendent of the Sussex County Department of Weights and Measures. "I don't know if that was the right thing to do, but that's the way we did it."

A big part was persuading their two sons, Terry and David, to help them. When the Heaters bought the diner, Terry, who has a degree in accounting, was about to graduate.

"I said, 'You need experience. Why don't you do the books here?'" Linda recalls. "He ended up cooking."

The boys cook, Mom makes the soups and helps cook, and Dad does whatever needs to be done.

The diner opens at 5:00 A.M. every day, even Sundays. Hunting and fishing are big up here, and the diner is an hour from the Poconos.

"In hunting and fishing season, it's wall to wall in here," Linda says. "They depend on us to open up."

"We put in new windows—they were leaking," Jerry continues. "We had to put in new air-conditioning, stainless-steel tables in back. We tore the floor up, put in a new floor. Put in more modern soda and juice machines."

Despite the up-to-date equipment, the diner has a decidedly country atmosphere, with the green-and-yellow interior and the rural surroundings, including a huge parking lot. There are county maps on either side of the door, something seen at too few diners.

Pancakes and waffles are popular at the Five Star, but Linda has made a name with her soups. Hearty Italian minestrone. Split pea. Mushroom-barley. Tomato-crab bisque. Carrot chowder.

How many different soups are there?

"Oh gee, fifty or sixty," says Jerry, eyes lighting up like a little kid's. "I can eat any of them."

"But breakfast is the main thing," Linda says. "Home fries are from scratch. We cut them and deep-fry them ourselves."

"We go through several hundred pounds of potatoes a week," Jerry chimes in. "Home fries—they don't get a couple slices but a whole big scoop."

For a customer who just had bypass surgery, they made something called Turkey Surprise—sliced turkey on a bed of fresh fruit and vegetables. Other customers started asking for it, so the Heaters put it on the menu.

Terry and David now own part of the Five Star, and Linda says they can do what they want with the diner—"keep it or sell it."

"I mow the grass, fill the holes in the driveway, patch the roof," says Jerry, his job description reaching epic lengths. "There never seems to be enough time to do what we have to do."

"Every week, we pick out one more thing to do," Linda says. "We've done the painting . . ."

"We did a *lot* here," Jerry says, as if only now realizing it. "They let it go to pot. It just needed some tender loving care."

Five Star Diner, Branchville.

EGGS OVER

wo eggs over (you like them sunny side up, fine), home fries, toast, and coffee. It is the most basic diner meal, the primal breakfast, if you will.

Whole wheat instead of white? Sure.

Any of us could make this at home for about a dollar, but for some reason we must have someone else make it and charge us four bucks besides.

Two eggs with bacon at a popular South Jersey diner: $5.50. Not including tip.

Amazingly, plenty of diners can't even make eggs right.

One of my favorite breakfasts is bacon and egg on a hard roll. Do you know how many times I've ordered it at a diner and ended up with a shriveled-up egg and a puny strip of bacon in a stale little roll?

That'll be $3.75, please.

Some diners do it right: The Liberty Diner on Route 130 in North Brunswick offers the best bacon and egg on a hard roll I've ever had. Not far behind: the Wildwood Diner, the Cup and Saucer in Paulsboro, and the Burlington Diner. Love that toasted roll at the last.

Which brings us to Primal Breakfast Rule Number One: Order eggs only in a diner that knows how to cook them.

Two places immediately come to mind: The Short Stop in Bloomfield, home of Eggs-in-the-Skillet, and the Egg Platter in Paterson.

You just know, by the names, you're not going to go wrong.

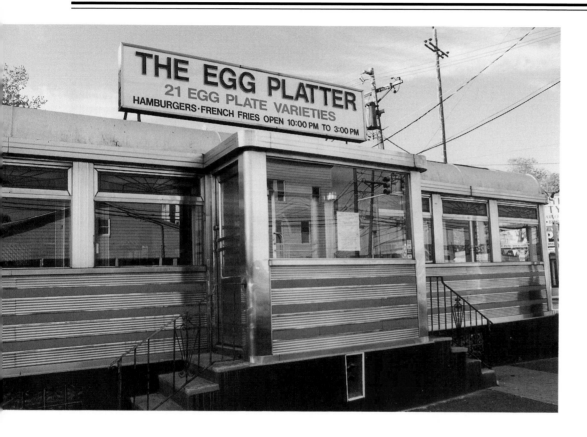

The Egg Platter on Crooks Avenue in Paterson offers twenty-one egg plate "varieties" or "novelties" (whichever word you prefer).

◆ ◆ ◆ 👑 ◆ ◆ ◆

"Wait a minute," you ask, "Paterson?" Yes, though Paterson is a shadow of its former prosperous self (in 1900 it was the fifteenth largest city in the United States).

There's still a lot worth knowing, and seeing. Native sons include Albert Sabin, who developed oral polio vaccine; Larry Doby, the first African American to play in the American League; poet Allen Ginsberg; and Lou Costello. Yes, of Abbott and Costello. Poet William Carlos Williams was born in Rutherford, but he'll always be associated with Paterson because of his poem of the same name.

TWENTY ONE
1. TWO EGGS *ANY STYLE* 1.60
2. HAM & EGGS 3.35
3. BACON & EGGS 3.35
4. SAUSAGE & EGGS 3.35
5. TAYLOR HAM & EGGS 3.35
6. PASTRAMI & EGGS 3.95
7. CORNED BEEF HASH & EGGS 4.35

EGG PLATTER
8. PLAIN OMELETTE 1.80
9. JELLY OMELETTE 2.95
10. CHEESE OMELETTE 3.50
11. HAM & CHEESE OMELETTE 4.45
12. HAM OMELETTE 3.85
13. WESTERN OMELETTE 3.95
14. FETA CHEESE OMELETTE 4.50

NOVELTIES
15. MUSHROOM OMELETTE 4.25
16. SPANISH OMELETTE 3.95
17. ONION OMELETTE 2.95
18. POTATO & ONION OMELETTE 3.45
19. SPANISH WESTERN OMELETTE 4.95
20. WESTERN PARMEGIAN 4.95
21. SPANISH PARMEGIAN 4.85

Forget twenty-one. At the Egg Platter anything is possible. Jelly omelette? Sure. Cream-cheese omelette? Coming right up.

At nineteen the Egg Platter's Spiro Dermatis may be the youngest diner manager in the state.

Paterson still has the Great Falls of the Passaic River, and the Paterson Museum, and, of course, the Egg Platter, on Crooks Avenue. And don't forget Chappy's, another classic diner (see the "City Diners" chapter).

The sign outside the Egg Platter reads 21 EGG PLATE VARIETIES; a sign inside reads 21 EGG PLATTER NOVELTIES, and, given the choice, I'd rather have an egg variety than an egg novelty, but as it turns out they're one and the same.

Two eggs any style, $1.60, cooked on a grill right in front of you, served hot and sizzling. The coffee comes in one of those cheap white plastic cups with a cupholder, but hey, this is a blue-collar kind of place.

"Eggs, eggs, eggs, biggest seller is eggs," says manager Spiro Dermatis, who at nineteen may be the youngest diner manager in the state.

His dad, Tom (who has since died), bought the diner in 1978. Built by Master Diners in nearby Pequannock in 1942, it was first known as the Borderline Diner (Crooks Avenue divides Paterson and Clifton).

Spiro says that the stainless-steel door and pink Formica counter were replaced and an eleven-table dining room added, but other than that, "What you see is what was here fifty years ago."

The Hamilton Beach milk shake machine has been in the diner "since the beginning of time," he says.

Actually you can get more than twenty-one different egg novelties at the Egg Platter. Someone once asked for a jelly omelette. No problem. Cream-cheese omelette? Piece of cake.

"Anything you want, we'll mix together for you in the kitchen," says Spiro, who is studying bookkeeping at Morris County College.

The Egg Platter's most popular breakfast? Eggs over easy, home fries, and toast.

And how many eggs does the Egg Platter go through in a week?

About fifteen cases. There are thirty dozen to a case, which means about 5,500 eggs a week.

"Lot of eggs," Spiro says.

◆ ◆ ◆ 🐛 ◆ ◆ ◆

Rule Number One for enjoying your Eggs-in-the-Skillet at the Short Stop in Bloomfield: Do not—repeat, do not—remove them from the skillet.

The eggs are served in a skillet, which is placed on a wooden trivet.

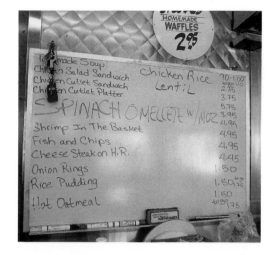

The Egg Platter, Paterson.

First and only rule at the Short Stop: Do not slide the eggs from the pan onto the wooden trivet. Believe it or not, some people have.

The Egg Platter, Paterson.

Omelettes, Wildwood Diner.

Some first-time customers have taken the skillet and dumped the eggs onto the trivet. Bad move. Studies have shown that eggs taste better in a hot, sizzling pan than on a cold wooden board.

"My first breakfast after I got out of the service was eggs in a skillet here," says regular Vince Sabato. "I didn't even know what a skillet was."

The Manno Dining Car diner, with its funky blue, green, red, yellow, and orange diagonal stripes, was one of five Short Stops. There were two in Newark, one in Plainfield, one in Belleville, and one in Bloomfield, which is the only one left in New Jersey. The Belleville Short Stop is now in Cleveland; its owner, Steve Harwin, is profiled in the "Steve and Jerry" chapter.

Denise Feliciano is the manager; her father, Richard Doyle, was a cook here for twenty-five years. Her sister, Donna, works here and even met her future husband at the Short Stop. The owners are Mary and Fred Turnbull.

"It's busy all the time," Denise says. "And they eat breakfast all the time. Two o'clock in the afternoon, they're eating pancakes."

Also available: the He-Man Cheese Omelette—three eggs, cheddar cheese, "golden" hash browns, lettuce and tomato, and toast and jelly.

Not filling enough? Try the Rib Sticker—a half pound of choice chopped sirloin, with hash browns and the rest.

"We're known for the best hamburgers," Denise says.

"Put it this way," adds cook Lee Slingerland, who has the ultimate short-order-cook name. "You eat a burger here and then go to McDonald's . . ."

"You'll never go there again," says Denise, finishing the sentence.

You wouldn't expect good coffee in a high-turnover place like this, but it's good and strong. This may be heresy, but not every diner serves good coffee. Too many serve a weak, watery brew. A Turkish proverb goes, "Coffee should be black as hell, strong as death, and sweet as love." I agree with that wholeheartedly, except I go easy on the sugar.

The Short Stop may look like a greasy spoon, but it pays attention to details. For example, Taylor Pork Roll, not some cheaper brand, is used.

"Pure butter, too," Denise says. "We have no freezer. Everything is fresh."

To cut costs, there are no single-serve packets of cream, ketchup, or mustard. No menus or checks either.

But if you order eggs at the Short Stop, just remember one thing: Keep them in the skillet.

Vince Sabato, a Short Stop regular who swears by the burgers and the coffee.

A SIDE ORDER OF HISTORY

The story of diners in New Jersey begins on sidewalks and street corners just after the turn of the century.

Jersey entrepreneurs, encouraged by the success of lunch wagons in New England, started building similar ones in Newark, Elizabeth, and elsewhere. "Fresh Eggs from Our Own Farm!" proclaimed a message on a lunch wagon in Plainfield around 1910.

As Richard J. S. Gutman explains in *American Diner Then and Now* (Harper-Collins, 1993), the diner business can be traced back to one Walter Scott, who set up his horse-drawn lunch cart on the streets of Providence, Rhode Island, in 1872.

Scott served boiled eggs with a slice of bread for a nickel, a plate of sliced chicken for thirty cents, and something called a "chewed sandwich"—scraps left over on the cutting board, chopped even finer, and spread with butter or mustard between two slices of bread.

The first walk-in lunch wagon appeared around 1884; in 1889 Charles H. Palmer of Worcester, Massachusetts, started building what he called "fancy night cafés" and "night lunch wagons"—most of the business was at night, after other restaurants closed.

Then came T. H. Buckley, the "Lunch Wagon King," who set up wagons in nearly three hundred towns across the country between 1893 and 1898.

The wagons would later be located on permanent sites, without wheels, and then became bigger, fancier, and more like diners as we know them today. Jerry O'Mahony started building diners in a Bayonne garage in 1913; P. J. Tierney Sons Inc. opened a plant in New Rochelle, New York, in 1925; and the diner industry was off and running.

Opposite: Marbett's, a White Tower, Camden.
(Courtesy of White Tower Corporation)

Lunch cart, early 1900s, unknown New Jersey location. (Courtesy of Herb Enyart)

◆ ◆ ◆ ♔ ◆ ◆ ◆

When he came home from the war, Tony Krilavicius opened a little diner at the corner of Frelinghuysen Avenue and Meeker Street in Newark, across from Weequahic Park.

Not World War II, World War I.

"When we first moved there, there was no airport there," Adele Yuknus Olesen, his stepdaughter, recalls. "Just dumps. They used to get around by horse and wagon."

In 1918 her stepfather opened Tony's Lunch. Raised off the ground—you'd climb up wooden steps to get inside—it looked like a real train car. Adele still has snapshots of the little diner. A man stands behind the counter at one end; two men are perched on uncomfortable-looking metal stools.

In 1926 Tony opened a larger diner, a storefront in a nearby building. It lasted until 1960. The 1926 menu and prices are visible in one of Adele's snapshots:

Special sirloin beef, *30 cents*
Rice pudding, *15 cents*
Veal Fricasse, *25 cents*

Adele worked there as a child, putting out napkins and cleaning up.

Her Lithuanian stepfather liked the bigger place, but there was a special place in his heart for the original Tony's Lunch.

"He was so proud of his little diner," Adele says.

◆ ◆ ◆ ❦ ◆ ◆ ◆

The builder of Tony's Lunch is unknown. But diners caught on so fast that by the 1940s there were about twenty different diner builders.

Today only four remain: Kullman Industries in Woodbridge; Sunrise Diner Manufacturers Inc. in Carteret; Paramount Modular Concepts in Oakland, Bergen County; and DeRaffele Manufacturing Co. in New Rochelle, New York.

"There's other companies building diners but they don't have the engineering we do," says Harold Kullman. "They come here, try to copy us."

"We're so far ahead of these guys it takes them a while to catch up," Phil DeRaffele says with a smile.

Though Herb Enyart, president of Paramount Modular Concepts, stays out of the who's-copying-whom game, he is quick to draw a line between his company and Kullman. "Our prices are relatively lower than Kullman," he says. "He's a big business. We manage to survive and be competitive."

As for the fourth company in the picture, Sunrise, the others pretend it doesn't exist. Owned by Ralph Musi, who started Musi Dining Car Co. in the mid-sixties, Sunrise concentrates on restoring older diners for overseas buyers.

"I don't know about them," Harold Kullman replies when asked about Sunrise and Musi.

"Is there bad blood between you two?"

"Bad history," he says. "I don't want to talk about it. I don't know where he is."

Tony's Lunch, which opened in 1918 across from Weequahic Park in Newark. (Courtesy of Adele Yuknus Olesen)

Today's BIGGEST DOLLAR Value!

Terra Cotta Design

Fluted Porcelain Design

Modernistic Design

Nowhere in America can you buy more diner per dollar than at Fodero

THIS IS WHAT YOU GET:

Sizes from 16' x 40' to 16' x 60'.

Undercarriage, frame, side supports, roof rafters of heavy gauge steel structure for extra strength.

All lumber of first quality, prime seasoned oak, spruce, and mahogany, treated to prevent warping.

Exterior of porcelain enamel trim with heavy gauge stainless steel. Doors of Formica or stainless steel.

All windows patented never-warp construction; aluminum sash frames; screens of aluminum.

Rock wool insulation used throughout the entire diner to insure warmth in winter, coolness in summer.

Heavy duty suction exhaust fans in roof at each end of diner eliminate odors and stale air.

Roof, of copper and lead finished tin, guaranteed against leaks for the lifetime of your diner.

Entire ceiling of the finest grade Formica in various colors.

Burn-proof, acid-resisting, durable Formica used for counter and table-tops.

Back wall of high polished heavy gauge stainless steel in various designs.

Side walls, counter front and floor of finest quality, long life tile. (Side walls tiled to level of windows; Formica to ceiling).

Spacious, roomy booths of burn-proof, grease-resisting leatherette or similar material.

Stools are chromium base and stand, bolted through the floor to guarantee no wobbling. Seat of chromium and leather; hair-filled padding.

Hood: completely heavy gauge stainless steel with menu boards built in.

Reach-in refrigerator, constructed of heavy gauge stainless steel interior and exterior with 4" cork insulation; steam table, salad display cases, sinks, shelving, etc., are all of the finest heavy gauge high polished stainless steel.

All equipment dimensions built to individual specifications.

Urns, deep fat fryers, broiler-griddle — optional at no extra cost.

Stainless steel, rust-resisting screws used throughout the entire diner. Highest quality door locks and door checks.

FODERO DINING CAR COMPANY

55 Delancey Street   Phone MArket 3-4917   **Newark 5, N. J.**

Fodero ad, The Diner, *July 1949.*

Paramount Diner plant, Haledon. (Courtesy of Herb Enyart)

PARAMOUNT
BUILDERS OF DINING CARS WITH A REPUTATION
Dining Cars
450 BELMONT AVE. HALEDON N.J.
TELEPHONE SHERWOOD 2-9025

January 7, 1941

Mr. Ernest Taylor and Peter Demopulos,
3 East Broad Street,
Hazelton, Pennsylvania.

Gentlemen:-

In accordance with our contract of January 6, 1941
this is to advise that we have proceeded with the construction
of 28' x 60' Diner with Dining Room and Kitchen at a purchase
price of $27,000.00 F.O.B. Factory. We agree to pay for
delivery of same.

A deposit of $3500.00 receipt of which is
hereby acknowledged and $3500.00 to be paid upon completion,
leaving a mortgage of $20,000.00 which is to be paid in
the following manner:-

12	Monthly installments @ $400.00 -	$4800.00
12	" " @ $450.00 -	$5400.00
11	" " @ $500.00 -	$5500.00
1	Final "	$4300.00
	Total	$20000.00

All materials and workmanship in accordance
with the best standard practice in dining car building.

Thanking you for this order and assuring you
of complete satisfaction, we are

Very truly yours,

PARAMOUNT DINERS, INC.

Arthur E. Sieber
A. E. Sieber, Pres.

Paramount contract, 1941. (Courtesy of Herb Enyart)

The late, great Julie's Diner, Route 46, Denville.

Julie's Diner.

Which is interesting, since Musi's plant is located ten minutes from Kullman Industries.

Ralph Musi, incidentally, once worked at Kullman.

◆ ◆ ◆ 👑 ◆ ◆ ◆

Samuel Kullman, Harold's father, started the company in 1927, on Frelinghuysen Avenue in Newark. Kullman had been the accountant at P. J. Tierney. When he left Tierney, he persuaded Joseph Fodero, metal shop foreman at Tierney, to go with him. Fodero would later open the Fodero Dining Car Co.

When Samuel Kullman worked at Tierney, the company was building "very small roadside diners catering to truckers, no women allowed," Harold Kullman recalls. The

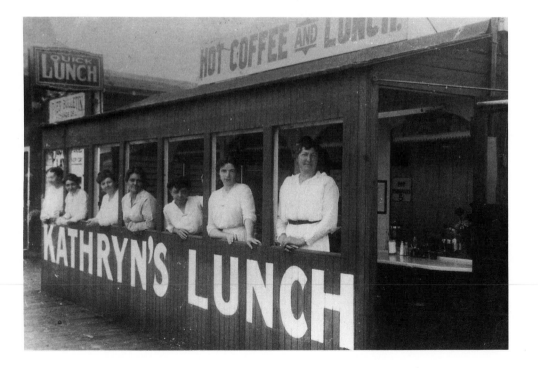

Kathryn's Lunch, a railroad car-like diner probably in New England, circa 1920.
(Courtesy of Don Preziosi)

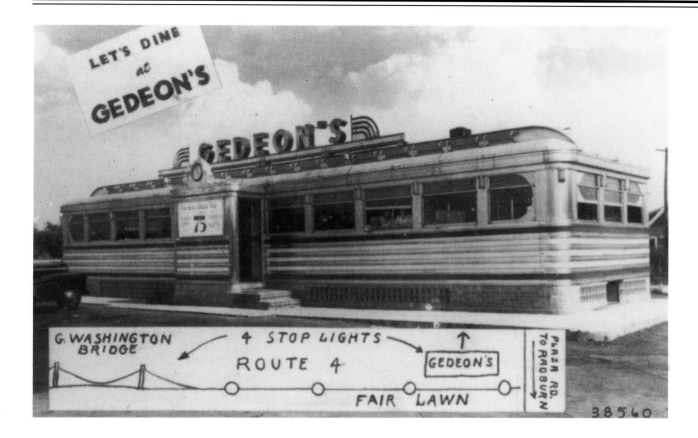

LET'S DINE
at
GEDEON'S

GEDEON'S

G. WASHINGTON BRIDGE — 4 STOP LIGHTS — ↑ GEDEON'S
ROUTE 4
FAIR LAWN
PLAZA RD. TO RADBURN
38560

company liked Samuel Kullman so much it bought him a Packard and built him a house. As soon as the house was finished, Kullman sold it and used the money to start his own business, according to his son.

Harold Kullman doesn't know his father's first diner—"I should have asked him a long time ago." He joined the family business in 1947 as a salesman.

"When I started, diners were sold by the running foot, like boats," Harold Kullman explains. "It was about four hundred dollars a running foot, so a sixty-foot diner cost twenty-four thousand dollars. Sixteen thousand dollars, you could buy a diner. Today you could buy a dishwasher with that."

A crude but effective map helped motorists find their way to Gedeon's Diner in Fair Lawn. (Courtesy of Don Preziosi)

Jack's Quick Lunch, Hoboken. (Courtesy of Christine Guedon-DeConcini)

Today a Kullman diner costs about three hundred dollars per square foot. A twenty-four-by-sixty-foot unit, for example, would cost $432,000 from the factory.

"And then you've got to buy a twenty-four-by-sixty kitchen and a twenty-four-by-sixty dining room," Kullman adds.

Until 1969 diners constituted 100 percent of the company's business. In the early seventies, Kullman Industries branched out into a new business—modular buildings—schools, jails, clinics, and communications facilities. Today diners constitute just 20 percent of the company's business.

"It is so costly to build a diner these days," Kullman says. "There are very few people who can afford to go into the business anymore. The site can need anywhere from four hundred thousand to one million dollars [in necessary improvements] before you can even bring the diner in."

Yet any diner, with the "right operator," will make money, he says.

"We found [that] the best place to put a diner," he adds, "is in the middle of a whole group of restaurants. My favorite location is right next to a McDonald's or Burger King. How many hamburgers can you eat?"

◆ ◆ ◆ ♛ ◆ ◆ ◆

A decade-by-decade summary of diners in America, according to diner authority Richard J. S. Gutman:

1920s: The first boom period for dining cars, which sprang up along the roadside to feed drivers flooding the new highways.

1930s: The emergence of such new materials as Formica, glass block, and stainless steel, which were immediately put to use in diner construction.

In the early 1930s, Art Sieber, president of Paramount Diners, invited sheet-metal worker Erwin Senior to the plant to make some stainless steel coffee urns. Senior noticed a diner under construction and told Sieber that a little stainless would look good in it. Sieber agreed, and had a worker bend some stainless for window trim.

Other diner builders took notice, and soon stainless, a tough, durable metal, replaced tile as the wall surface of choice. Stainless spread to the outside of diners, and the combination of stainless steel and porcelain enamel resulted in "the most eye-catching, colorful diners of all time," Gutman says.

Formica-brand laminate was invented in 1913 but didn't find its way into diners until the mid-1930s, Gutman explains. It was first used to insulate industrial products from acids, oils, and the like—thus the name *for mica,* "used in place of mica." By 1940, there were seventy colors of Formica to choose from.

1940s: The golden age. Diners were long, low, "fluid looking" structures with no hard edges; all corners were rounded. One design trademark of this time: the generous use of reflective surfaces.

1950s: Diners move to the suburbs, and their grills move behind closed doors, into the kitchen. The "railroad" look is replaced by a "wide-open" look, with large picture windows.

1960s: The futuristic age of diners, with zigzag roofs and flared canopies.

1970s: The Mediterranean style is the dominant look, with its palazzo of stone surmounted by a Spanish-quarry-tile mansard roof. The king of the Mediterranean-diner builders: DeRaffele Manufacturing Co. of New Rochelle, New York.

"Right now," Phil DeRaffele says over a drawing board, "we're sort of running out of things to do with these diners."

You can bet that DeRaffele and his designers, and their counterparts at Kullman and Paramount Modular, will think of something before long, though.

"I'm working on something now," DeRaffele says conspiratorially, "that is unbelievable."

Opposite: A Victory Day parade rolls past the Reo Diner in Woodbridge in 1946. (Courtesy of the Reo Diner)

Francis Dolbow

Jim Burley

Jack Berry

The Elite Diner was located at 235 E. Broadway, Salem, N. J. from 1926 to 1963. Originally owned by Mrs. Thorpe from 1926-28. Owned by Jack Berry 1928-57. Owned by Skinny Dean 1957-59. Owned by Jim Burley 1959-61. The last ones to run the diner from 1961-63 were Bob & Barbara McAllister. The diner was moved to make way for The Salem Motor Lodge.

The former Elite Diner, Salem. (Courtesy of Barb and Bob McAllister)

What it is he won't tell, especially to a reporter who plans to interview his competitors.

In the thirties, his father, Angelo, and Carl Johnson, a former carpenter and president of P. J. Tierney, respectively, started building diners under the name Johnson & DeRaffele. In 1947 Angelo DeRaffele became sole owner. On the death of his father in 1954, Phil DeRaffele became president.

He's not one to wax romantic about classic stainless-steel diners. For the nineties diner manufacturer, bigger is the only better.

"If you ask me if I like the old diners, I would say no," he explains. "Sure, the workmanship, the stainless steel, was nice, but the floor plan, the operation, was terrible."

In the 1940s and 1950s, diner manufacturers vied with one another to see who could build the world's largest diner. Just being different was a mark of pride. DeRaffele built what some consider to be the world's smallest modern diner, the Night Owl, in Providence.

DeRaffele makes more diners than either Kullman or Paramount Modular, although most of its business is in Long Island. The company's Jersey diners include the Hightstown, Burlington, and Olga's.

How are diner designs chosen? At DeRaffele a prospective owner will generally check out existing diners and tell Phil which one he'd like his diner to resemble.

"They'll like 70 percent of one and maybe 30 percent of another," he explains. "They sort of approve the color scheme, the light fixtures. They have the choice of equipment. . . . Everyone has a different idea of the operation. Some want the fryer next to the steam table, some want the fryer next to the broiler."

His theory on why there are so many Greeks in the diner business: "Originally diner operators were Italian, German, Jewish, Swiss, everything but Greek. When they came here, the best jobs were in diners or restaurants, washing dishes. Once they became the owners, new immigrants would come to work for them."

Phil says that thirty, forty years ago one could tell who built what diner. Today that's no longer the case.

"So how do you tell the difference between a DeRaffele and another company's?"

He grins. "It's the most beautiful thing in the world."

❖ ❖ ❖ 👑 ❖ ❖ ❖

Herb Enyart doesn't mind playing the much-smaller brother, businesswise, to Kullman and DeRaffele.

"There's a lot of work out there," the president of Paramount Modular Concepts says in his spacious but sparsely furnished office. "The point is, how deep do you want to get in, how many headaches do you want?"

The sixty-one-year-old executive keeps his headaches to a minimum; PMC, as it is known, builds about a half dozen diners every year. The company is a spinoff of Paramount Diners, founded by Arthur Sieber in 1932. The original company—responsible for Rosie's, once of Little Ferry, the Turnabout in Phillipsburg, and the famed Melrose in Philadelphia—closed its doors in the early seventies.

"The most luxurious and comfortable air-conditioned diner in the world," according to the words across the facade, the Queen Mary was the only "ferry diner" in history. It was located somewhere along the Jersey coast. This photo was taken in the late 1930s. (Courtesy of Don Preziosi)

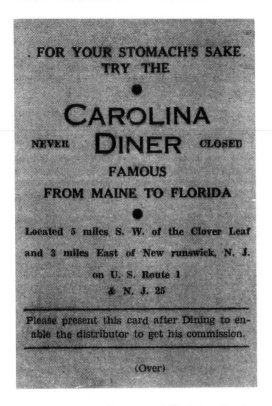

Carolina Diner. (Courtesy of Christine Guedon-DeConcini)

Enyart, who, like Sieber, worked at Silk City, bought the equipment and machinery. There are only a dozen employees at PMC; some of the work is subcontracted.

"We just shipped this here classical job," Enyart says of the Eveready Diner in Hyde Park, New York. "This was number 174."

The Eveready is done in what he calls a "classical Art Deco" style. PMC's Jersey diners include the Stateline in Mahwah, the Coach House in North Bergen, and the Nevada in Bloomfield.

Enyart started as a carpenter at the Paterson Vehicle Co., familiarly known as Silk City for its line of diners. You saw one Silk City, you saw them all, because the diners were built as quickly and as economically as possible.

"I do all the designing myself, the calculations," he says of PMC's diners. "I'm not an engineer. It's just plain simple know-how."

The company makes its own furniture—"it doesn't come off the shelf," Enyart notes—and prides itself on handling unusual assignments. It renovated Willie's Diner in Bloomfield, giving the old Fodero diner a mirrorlike stainless-steel front.

Another job involved building an addition to a Staten Island diner, including an elevated section with parking underneath.

"Crazy jobs," Enyart says, smiling. "We seem to get the difficult ones. Makes it interesting."

◆ ◆ ◆  ◆ ◆ ◆

When Pat Fodero used to meet with prospective diner owners, he would excuse himself, go out to his car, and bring back a bottle of aspirin and some water.

"What's that for?" the curious owner would ask.

"When you hear our price," Fodero would say, "you're going to need it."

Fodero diners cost more than the competition, but you got more.

Joe Fodero, Pat's father, started the company in 1933 on Oakwood Avenue in Bloomfield. Fodero had worked at P. J. Tierney as metal shop foreman, making griddles and coffee urns, and then at Kullman.

"He built his first diners in a side lot at his home," recalls Pat Fodero, who was ten years old at the time. "He used the garage as a workshop. We had no complaints from the neighbors."

Baltimore Diner, Route 1, New Brunswick. (Courtesy of Marvin Krupnick)

In the late thirties, Fodero moved his operation to a plant on Delancey Street in Newark. The famed Empire Diner, in New York City, was built at the Newark plant. In 1950 the company moved again, to Bloomfield.

"Even during the depression, the diners did pretty good," Fodero says. "They sold you a bowl of soup for a nickel."

The company was known for the decorative work in its diners.

"A stainless-steel clock was our emblem," he observes. "If you saw that, you knew it was a Fodero."

In the forties the company built four diners at a time in its factory, employing forty steady workers and many subcontractors. The average diner length was about twenty-nine feet. Average cost, about $30,000.

The boom years, however, came in the fifties and sixties.

"We were really knocking them out," Fodero recalls. "The seventies weren't bad, but there were a lot more restrictions. The most profitable by far were the fifties."

Stanley's Ideal Diner, Keyport, 1920s. The wooden diner was replaced by a stainless-steel one around 1950. It is now called the Seaport Diner. (Courtesy of the Seaport Diner and Tim Ferrante)

In 1967 the Forum Diner, a Fodero, was built on Route 4 in Paramus.

"Money was no object; it was a showpiece," he says. "Everybody said it would be a big white elephant. But people didn't realize that big was the way business was being done."

Fodero's Jersey diners include Tops Diner in East Newark, Geets Diner in Williamstown, and the Rustic Mill Diner in Cranford.

Rising interest rates, Fodero says, forced the company to close in 1981. Joseph Fodero died in 1989 at the age of ninety-two. Pat Fodero doesn't build diners anymore, he designs them, through Americana Diner Consultants in Camarillo, California. But he remembers when Fodero was a name in the diner business.

Once he was about to close a deal with a client on a $223,000 diner. Suddenly, the client started sweating profusely.

"He looked like he was going to have a heart attack," Fodero recalls. "I asked, 'What's wrong?' He said, 'I don't like that three, change it to a two or four.' He was superstitious." Fodero laughs. "I changed it to a four."

◆ ◆ ◆ 👑 ◆ ◆ ◆

Ralph Musi is not surprised when told about Harold Kullman's reaction to the mention of his name.

"I was the plant supervisor (at Kullman Dining Car Co.)," Musi says. "Harold always promised me that when his father retired I would get shares of the business. I got nothing. So I left, went on my own.

"At first I was his best man in the world. When I left I was the worst. He knocked me down, I knocked him down. There was a war."

Wayside Diner. (Courtesy of Marvin Krupnick)

Musi, who emigrated from Italy in 1947, formed the Musi Dining Car Co. in 1966. He remembers how important P. J. Tierney was to the beginning of the New Jersey diner industry. Angelo DeRaffele (Phil DeRaffele's father), Jerry O'Mahony (founder of Jerry O'Mahony Inc.), Joe Fodero (founder of Fodero Dining Car Co.), and Samuel Kullman all worked there.

Jerry Campora, Musi's father-in-law, worked for Kullman and then started his own dining car company.

He and Harold Kullman may not like each other, but Musi liked Samuel Kullman.

"The old man was good; he was strictly business," he recalls. "He used to sing a lot. I know when Sam Kullman sings, there's a problem.

While Harold Kullman dresses in fine suits, his former associate wears an old blue windbreaker, and there is grease under his nails. Kullman has carpeting in his modern office, Musi an old tile floor in his shop office.

Musi spends most of his time restoring old or abandoned diners and selling them to buyers overseas. The Fat Boy chain of fast-food restaurants has bought five, including the former Plaza View in Jersey City, and relocated them in and around London. One of the five, the Boulevard Diner in Queens, had bullet holes in the exterior walls from an attempted gangland hit. Musi kept them in; the Fat Boy people loved it.

Musi's newest idea: diners in shopping-center parking lots. Musi is negotiating with the owner of a Monmouth County shopping center.

"Every shopping center should have a diner," he says. "I don't care where you put it, on the side, in front. I'm telling you, it will go like hotcakes. People will go shopping, go in diner, go home."

WILDWOOD DINER, 9 A.M.

The two men and three college students are performing a ballet of sorts in the kitchen.

A hand swoops over the grill, breaking a couple of eggs.

A body hops sideways; pancakes have to be flipped.

Two feet glide toward the refrigerator; more cheese is needed.

A hand grabs a plate and sets it on the counter with a clatter.

Another hand reaches into a microwave, pulls something out.

"Give me a western omelette, cheese omelette, stack, short stack," a man with a black cowboy hat shouts.

"Sausage, I got plenty of it," announces a younger man, pulling a basket from the deep-fryer.

The place is the kitchen of the Wildwood Diner; the time, Sunday morning, the busiest day of the week for this diner, any diner.

"Twenty-one over, put on a stack," the man with the cowboy hat says.

"Stack," one of the college kids repeats.

"I need two pork roll and egg and cheese."

The man in the cowboy hat is Ken Smith. He's the head cook. The guy by the fryer basket is Joe Scrocca, whom everyone calls Jay. He's the boss. His parents, Joe and Delores, have owned the diner since 1957.

It is a Sunday morning in the middle of the summer, which for a shore diner means only one thing.

Hey, pardner, how about a western omelette? Chief cook Ken Smith, with his familiar cowboy hat, behind the grill of the Wildwood Diner.

Joe "Jay" Scrocca ("I'll drop thirty pounds in the summer") runs the Wildwood Diner.

Maureen McCormick performs a balancing act at the Wildwood Diner.

Bedlam.

"Short stack, tomato omelette, mushroom and cheddar—two tomato omelettes—ham, cheddar and onion."

"Twenty-one over."

"Give me those omelettes again. There's something there with mushrooms."

No codes are used here; twenty-one—two eggs on one plate—is about as complicated as it gets (forty-two is four eggs on two plates).

Today Jay—"I do whatever they need"—is doing eggs. One of the college kids is doing pancakes, another French toast. Smith takes the waitresses' orders, cooks, and announces finished orders into a microphone hooked up to a PA system in the dining rooms.

It is already ninety degrees outside, and inside the kitchen it is hotter than diner hell.

"I enjoy it," says Jay, drenched in sweat. "This is my workout. I drop thirty pounds in the summer."

Not long ago he thought his career path was set, and it didn't go through diners. He had worked at the diner since he was six; they'd set up a stool for him so he could remove glasses from the dishwasher. He went to college, though, to become an accountant.

But when his mother needed help at the diner, he came aboard full-time and sold his accounting practice.

"I pride myself as being one of the few short-order cooks in the country with a degree in accounting and a master's in tax law," he says.

"I've worked in a lot of diners," Ken says. "This is a well-run machine. No one runs as efficiently as this one, no one has the production this one has."

The pancake guy does pancakes, the egg guy does eggs. The order slips get put right there, nowhere else. One guy is in charge. Nobody, literally or figuratively, steps on somebody else's toes.

"As busy as it gets, it runs smooth," Jay says. "You have a choice—make it run smooth or run out the back door."

Waitresses and waiters dart in and out of the door. A cardboard box goes sliding across the floor. A young girl makes toast; that's her job. She doesn't want her picture taken, as if having her friends see her at the toaster would be the worst thing that could happen to her.

"We lost an entire shift when the casinos came in," Jay says. "They created an entire industry—the bus industry. They'd bring you in and feed you, make sure you stayed down there."

The diner stayed open twenty-four hours until the mid-eighties. It is open just during the summer, although the definition of summer keeps getting stretched.

"We seem to stay open a couple weeks later every year," Jay says. "It's now about mid-April to the end of October."

The diner does not entirely shut down during the off-season, either. The family's pasta business, Molto Foods, operates year-round. It makes pasta for the diner and for area restaurants.

"Two bacon and cheddar, western and cheese, pepper and ham!" Ken yells. He looks quizzically at a check. "Western, no onions. How do you do that?"

In 1957 Joe Scrocca, Jay's dad, and several relatives bought the diner.

Wildwood Diner.

"Then it's not a western," Jay says.

Most popular item on Sunday? Omelette. Most popular omelette? "Anything with cheddar cheese," Ken says.

"Jimmy, can you get me a pack of cheddar out of the fridge?"

"For me, learning how to cook was like baptism by fire," Jay says during a rare lull. "I was just like everybody else. I got yelled at, I got screamed at, I left here crying."

"All right, boys," Ken says around 11:30 A.M. "Get your hamburger out. It's time for lunch."

But breakfast never ends. At noon there are more omelettes on the grill than hamburgers.

"Load the toaster. Gimme that cheeseburger. Gimme that English muffin."

"That club is dry, no tomatoes, BLT whole wheat toast?"

"I got it in."

"Fried onions on that deluxe?"

"Yeah."

"I wish I had a six-burner range," Jay says wistfully. "I wish I could do sautéed onions. It doesn't hurt us, not having it, but it would help us, if you can understand that."

A waitress walks to the pickup area and hesitates. "Can you make [spaghetti] sauce without any meat in it?" she asks.

"I was making marinara yesterday and nobody wanted it," Jay says, frowning.

"Should I wait for an answer?" the waitress asks in just the right tone of voice.

"Is Pop back there?" Jay asks Chico Velez, who has worked here thirty years. Chico nods his head.

"Is he in a good mood?"

"All right, listen up," Ken is saying. "I need a roast beef on rye and a club. That's a roast beef, no mayo. Can I have french fries?"

"They're cooking."

Standing next to the deep-fryer, with the grill to one side and heat everywhere, I feel like I'm about to evaporate.

"You think it's hot now, wait until tonight," Jay says. "You got the broiler going and these two burners and the hot fryers and the barbecue grill . . ."

"Hey, Kenny," a waitress asks. She wants to tell him a joke she heard this morning. "Do you know the difference between Wheaties and sex?"

Ken shakes his head.

"Let's go for breakfast," the waitress says.

"That wasn't even funny," he says after she leaves.

"It's in your blood," Jay says at 12:15. "In two weeks we'll be so tired and dragging we'll say we can't wait until the summer's over. A week after you close, you can't wait for it to open again."

Meatballs, Wildwood Diner.

STEVE AND JERRY

*A*merica's—and New Jersey's—most famous diner is located in, of all places, Michigan, on something called 14 Mile Road. There's no sign on the interstate; you just figure that since 12 Mile Road was back there a ways, this must be 14 Mile Road.

The road takes you to Rockford, which is halfway between Paris and Holland, or, if you prefer, Nirvana and Climax. If you miss 14 Mile Road, you might end up in Canada before you know it, because America's most famous diner is located smack in the middle, as its owner likes to say, "of frickin' nowhere."

Oh, yes. On the day I visited—rainy, cold, miserable—the parking lot was packed.

"Everyone told me I was nuts," a bearded Jerry Berta says of his moving Rosie's Diner, once the pride of Little Ferry, to western Michigan in 1991.

Today Rosie's is the star attraction of Diner World, aka Diner Land (Jerry is not quite sure what to call it), the nation's only diner theme park, which, unlike Disney World or Great Adventure, costs nothing to enter.

Unless you're hungry.

In the past four years, a lot of hungry, caffeine-crazed, and just plain curious folks have found Rosie's, adding to the fifty-year-old diner's legend.

A local restaurant owner recently grumbled, "The damn guy who owns Rosie's doesn't know a damn thing about running a diner and he can't turn people away."

The "damn guy" who owns Rosie's doesn't run it, which may be why the diner is packing them in.

"I'd be a horrible manager," Jerry, forty-five, says. "I'm an artist. I go from here to there. I have ideas."

Diner Land's owner, who looks like an aging hippie but talks like your teenage son, creates ceramic diner sculptures, on sale in the Diner Store located next to Rosie's. The Diner Store was originally Uncle Bob's Diner in Flint, Michigan. Jerry bought it in 1987 for two thousand dollars.

There are two more diners at Diner World. The Delux Diner, once Uncle Wally's in White Creek, New York, is an upscale diner with undinerlike dishes: tiger shrimp with bacon and cucumber and sherry-charbroiled pork loin, among others. The diner also includes the Dinerland Bakery.

The fourth diner is an addition to the Delux built by Berta and helpers. The Delux is a Silk City. The addition is a "Jerry-built," naturally.

More than half of the operating diners in Michigan—there are just seven—can be found within a cheeseburger's throw of one another at Diner World.

"I really don't know how to run a restaurant," Jerry insists. "But I know how to be a customer. Consistency is the biggest thing. Pancakes shouldn't be great one day and shitty the next."

And waitresses, in Jerry's diner anyway, shouldn't be happy one day and mopey the next.

Rosie's waitresses are so bubbly, you expect them to break into song at any moment.

"Yee hah!" one of them shouts above the midmorning din.

"Jerry," says another, spotting the owner at the counter. "Get your apron on, babe."

"If you're a waitress, this is great," Jerry says later. "Here you're the star."

◆ ◆ ◆ ♔ ◆ ◆ ◆

The Michigan native saw Rosie's on his first trip to New Jersey in 1979. On his way to a crafts fair, he drove by a diner he considered so perfect that it looked like the "Holy Grail." Rosie's. He got out of his car and started taking pictures; a cook ran out and told him he couldn't do that.

Ten years later he was at the White Manna in Hackensack—his favorite diner in the world—when he decided to visit Rosie's again. The diner was closed, but owner

Hot Sandwiches
Choose your favorite and we'll serve it up with REAL mashed potatoes, homemade gravy and your choice of vegetables, diner slaw or applesauce · 4.95
Roast Beef
Turkey · Hamburger
Diner-Made Meatloaf
Roast Pork

Rosie's BURGERS

Patty Melt
Our juicy third pound of beef on top of grilled rye bread, blanketed with Swiss cheese and sauteed onions; served with potato chips and pickles · 4.75
Make it a Basket... with French fries and diner slaw · 5.75

Mushroom Swiss Burger
Swiss cheese, sauteed mushrooms and onions top this juicy third-pound burger; served with lettuce, tomato, pickles and potato chips · 4.75
Make it a Basket... with French fries and diner slaw · 5.75

Olive Cheeseburger
American cheese and sliced green olives top this hearty third-pound burger. We'll also add lettuce, tomato, pickles and chips on the side · 4.75
Make it a Basket... with French fries and diner slaw · 5.75

Jerry Burger
Try something different... this juicy third-pound burger is topped with Swiss cheese, shaved ham, Thousand Island dressing, lettuce and tomato; served with potato chips · 4.75
Make it a Basket... with French fries and diner slaw · 5.75

Rosie's Burger
It's so juicy and delicious, you don't need the extras, but we'll add lettuce, tomato and pickles; served with potato chips · 5.95
Make it a Basket... with French fries and diner slaw · 4.95
Add cheese · .55 extra   Add bacon · .75 extra
Double the meat · 1.00 extra

The Platters

Grilled Chicken Sandwich
A tender breast of chicken grilled to its juicy best, accented with lettuce, tomato, mayo and pickles; sided with potato chips · 4.45
Make it a Basket... with French fries and diner slaw · 5.45

The Reuben Grill
Our lean deli corned beef is heaped on fresh rye with sauerkraut, Swiss cheese and our homemade Thousand Island dressing, then grilled; served with potato chips · 4.45
Make it a Basket... with French fries and diner slaw · 5.45

Fish Sandwich
Always a favorite. Flaky Alaskan cod fillet dipped in our delicious batter and fried golden; served on a club roll with lettuce and tartar sauce garnish. Sided with potato chips · 3.95
Make it a Basket... with French fries and diner slaw · 4.95

You Ain't Nothin' But a Hound Dog
Start with a foot long hot dog, sided with potato chips and served your way...
With Chili, Cheese and Onion · 3.75
Chicago-Style with tomato, onion, hot peppers and relish · 3.75
Make it a Basket... either of the above served with French fries and diner slaw · 4.75
Classic Dog & Chips · 2.95
Basket · 3.95

The Club
A triple-decker club sandwich with mayo, lettuce, tomato, bacon, turkey, ham and Swiss cheese; served with potato chips · 4.95
Make it a Basket... with French fries and diner slaw · 5.95

Grilled Ham & Cheese
Two kinds of cheese and deli ham between thick-sliced homemade bread, grilled golden; served with potato chips and pickles · 3.95
Make it a Basket... with French fries and diner slaw · 4.95

Meatball Sub
Pat's famous homemade meatballs served on a club roll with our zesty sauce and lots of mozzarella cheese; served with chips · 4.95
Make it a Basket... with French fries and diner slaw · 5.95

Country-Fried Steak Sandwich
Beef steak, pounded thin, breaded and fried golden brown... served on a bun with mayo, lettuce, tomatoes and pickles; sided with potato chips · 4.95
Make it a Basket... with French fries and diner slaw · 4.95

♦ GREY POUPON
DIJON MUSTARD

Menu, Rosie's Diner.

Jerry Berta, owner/impresario of Diner World, or Diner Land, the nation's only diner theme park.

Ralph Corrado happened to be around. Jerry showed him a postcard of Uncle Bob's, which he owned. "You want to buy another one?" Corrado asked. He had sold the lot, and had less than six weeks to sell Rosie's.

"It was fate," Jerry now says, "that drew me there."

He paid ten thousand dollars for Rosie's.

Originally the Silver Dollar Diner and the Farmland Diner, Rosie's acquired its name after the commercials for Bounty paper towels ("the quicker picker-upper"), featuring the late Nancy Walker, were filmed there.

"Welcome to the most famous diner in America," proclaims a vintage postcard of Rosie's, then located on the Route 46 circle in Little Ferry.

The diner, built by Paramount Diners in Haledon (now Paramount Modular Concepts in Oakland) was "full of trash" when Jerry bought it—not garbage trash, but trash such as video and cigarette machines and the awful avocado-colored counter Bounty installed for its commercials.

Jerry replaced all that and shipped the diner to its new home. Ten flat tires and an engine fire later, the truck made it to Rockford.

Rosie's owner knows more about diner operation than he lets on. When he opened Rosie's, he set a goal: a minimum of 101 meals served a day. If he could do that, he figured, he'd be okay.

"The first day, we had three hundred people," he recalls. "There was no publicity, nothing, just a sign outside."

It helped that he was a native son and that in Michigan the wheels of government seem to turn quicker than elsewhere.

"When we applied for a liquor license, it came in three days," he says.

The Diner Store carries Rosie's T-shirts, Rosie's postcards, Rosie's rulers, Jerry's porcelain diners (from about fifty to several thousand dollars) and artwork by his wife, Madeline Kaczmarczyk.

Jerry can usually be found in the store, working with assistant Fred Tiensivu in a kitchen-turned-studio amid a clutter of boxes and blueprints, or down in the basement, where he silk-screens T-shirts.

His diner sculptures have been bought by the likes of rocker Bob Seger and a former chairman of McDonald's. Jerry did a classic McDonald's for the latter, which required some swallowing of pride because he absolutely detests fast-food chains.

No false advertising here. The Diner Store sells artwork by Berta and his wife, Madeline Kaczmarczyk, plus Rosie's T-shirts, postcards, and pencils.

"We need more places like this that are not chains," he explains. "We need more individual things."

If you don't like the rides at a theme park, you can always eat. At Diner World, if you don't like to eat, you can always play miniature golf, on a course behind the Diner Store, where the obstacles are giant-size hamburgers, sausages, eggs sunny side up, and an overturned coffee cup, a tribute to Rosie's.

But wait, there's more, or soon will be. That weed-overgrown field behind the Diner Store? It will be turned into a volleyball court.

And the Delux—named after the Utica, Michigan, drive-in theater where Jerry saw *A Hard Day's Night* in the sixties—will serve "the best food in western Michigan," he claims.

"I know it's going to work," he says of his upscale diner. "You'll be treated right." He smiles. "This place is going to rock."

America's most famous diner—once New Jersey's—is already rocking. Rosie's makes the rest of Diner World possible.

"It's not like I take all the money and buy Porsches with it," Jerry says. "I drive an old van."

But don't let the humble act fool you. He talks about moving to Key West someday, and building a fish-shaped or some other outlandish-looking diner, like one of his sculptures.

Like P. T. Barnum, he is a tireless promoter. When *USA Today* wanted to install a newspaper box, Jerry said sure—as long as it wasn't bolted down. He wanted to be able to move it in case somebody had to do a photo shoot.

This guy may act like a free-spirited sixties dropout, but he doesn't miss a trick.

"It's cool, it's great, it faces the sunset," he says, surveying his kingdom. "It's like one big art project."

◆ ◆ ◆ ♛ ◆ ◆ ◆

The two diners sit at either end of the truck yard, one high up on blocks, worn and battered, the other as shiny and new as the day it left the factory back in 1949.

Somehow the two Jersey diners have made it here, to this truck yard in Cleveland.

There is a curly-haired man with white sneakers sitting in a booth at a third diner on blocks, accessible only by a rickety-looking ladder.

"I get a lot of people calling me about diners," he is saying. "There are a lot of dreamers out there."

Steve Harwin would consider himself a dreamer, but a wide-awake one. He is one of a handful of diner restorers in this country. The battered diner is the old Pole Tavern Diner, once on Route 40 in Upper Pittsgrove, Salem County. The shiny diner is the beloved Short Stop, formerly of Belleville.

"A lot of people talk about buying diners, but few go through with it," he says. "Few will risk it enough to jump into it. There are so many variables. [Bringing it up to construction] code can be a real pain. It's not just ten thousand dollars, twenty thousand dollars, buy the diner. You're talking big chunks of money. Three thousand dollars just to rig it . . ."

Diner restorer Steve Harwin in front of the old Pole Tavern Diner, once on Route 40 in Upper Pittsgrove, now on Harwin's lot in Cleveland.

What a mess! Restoring an old diner can take months. This is the interior of the Pole Tavern Diner.

An antique car buff, Steve would rescue cars from junk heaps and backyards and restore them. Friends in Europe kept telling him he should look into diners, so he did.

His first experience was not a pleasant one. He bought a 1941 Sterling Streamliner in Elmwood City, Pennsylvania, for twenty thousand dollars, moved it to Cleveland, saw it suffer severe wind damage in a storm, and sold it at a loss. It is now in Duluth, Minnesota.

His second experience was not much better. He bought the Hilltop Diner in Wrightstown, or thought he bought it, anyway. The 1955 Silk City diner was shipped to Ralph Musi's Sunrise Diner plant in Carteret for restoration and eventual shipment to London. Harwin was never paid the commissions due him, and took Musi to court. The diner still sits in Carteret. Steve says it's being held "hostage."

"I have not one good thing to say about Ralph; I won't say anything bad," he says. "I'm going to have to spend big money and go after big money. I hate the legal system, but I have no recourse."

Things have gone much better since. He bought the former East End Diner in Dover, a 1939 Silk City, and sold it to a Harley dealer in Grand Junction, Colorado. He bought the Short Stop and the Pole Tavern. He restored the Lafayette Diner in Easton, Pennsylvania; it is now in Connecticut.

After eight months of work he turned the former Ono Diner in Ono, Pennsylvania, into the Big Dig Diner, to be located at the entrance to Boston's Harbor Tunnel. It will be used as a vocational center for at-risk youth.

How did Ono get its name?

"The town fathers couldn't come up with a name. They kept arguing. That's how they came up with Ono."

He redesigned the diner's heating system; replaced the sliding windows with high-efficiency Thermopane glass; redid the roof; built a new counter; installed a new menu board, light fixtures, and stools; and brought the wiring up to code, among other things.

"It doesn't take a genius to do the work," the forty-five-year-old Cleveland native explains. "It just takes conscientiousness."

In his spare time he acts as a consultant to various restaurants and runs a series of crepe stands around Cleveland.

The Pole Tavern Diner, a rusted shell with a jumbled heap of metal and wood inside, is his next project. It is an early 1940s Silk City.

"If this thing lasted fifty years with nothing going in its favor, restore it, and there's no reason it shouldn't last twice as long."

The Pole Tavern, he says, will probably end up in California.

The American Diner—the one under the tarp over there—is destined for a spot near the Rock and Roll Museum downtown. It was an O'Mahony that went from Cleveland to Munster, Pennsylvania, and back to Cleveland.

The Short Stop is staying in Cleveland. He intends to lease the beautiful little diner with the distinctive orange flutes, but only to someone who promises to offer "real food—real hamburgers, real milkshakes . . ."

The Short Stop, he says, is not for sale.

Route 130 North, Carneys Point. Closed for several years, the diner was home of the seventy-two-ounce Honcho Special Steak.

We've heard about going out on the links, but this is ridiculous! Larger-than-life Fiberglas sausages are among the obstacles on the miniature golf course behind Rosie's.

"As soon as I saw it, I knew I had to have it," he adds. "The size, the color . . ." He laughs. "I consider this my mobile assault diner. We've thought about putting it on wheels and taking it to the Indy 500, the Kentucky Derby. It would do great business."

In the meantime he will climb up and down that rickety-looking ladder and bring these near-dead diners back to life.

"When this was built," he says, looking around the Big Dig Diner, "it was built with pride, it was built to last. Each diner carried its own individuality; it went right down to the roots. That's why diners have such an appeal today."

Fifth Avenue, Paterson.

NOT THAT SALEM OAK, THE OTHER SALEM OAK

Do diners run in the McAllister family or what? Back in the sixties, Bob and Ollie McAllister ran the Salem Oak Diner in Salem, at the same time their son, Bob, and his wife, Barbara, ran a diner, Bob's, up the street.

Bob junior probably welcomed the competition. After all, Bob senior was the one who docked his son four hours for leaving the Salem Oak early on his wedding day.

"He retired in 1965 and we took the diner over in 1967," Bob says of his father. "His retirement lasted about six weeks. He went to selling cars; sold them until the day he died."

It's a good bet that Bob and Barb will keep working in the Salem Oak until they can no longer pick up a menu or a spatula. Both fifty-eight—they were high school sweethearts—they have the energy and enthusiasm of people twenty years younger.

More important, they know the secret to a good diner marriage.

"The girls [waitresses] work for me, the boys [cooks] work for him," Barb says. "We have no problem."

While Barb is quiet and gracious, Bob is big and blustery. His usual outfit is the standard white diner pants and shirt, with multicolored suspenders.

"I might be here," he says of Tuesdays and Wednesdays, his days off, "but I won't talk to you. If you ask for me, I'll say, 'He's not here.'"

Tuesdays and Wednesdays, you see, are fishing days.

"The Good Lord covered this good earth with six times as much water as He did

Bob McAllister, co-owner, with his wife, Barbara, of the Salem Oak Diner.

Waitress Jennifer Ayars and J. R. Masters talk things over at the Salem Oak.

Salem Oak cook Roger Call can pour with the best of them.

land," he declares. "He meant for man to fish six times more than he works."

The Good Lord also meant for these two to be together. They were high school sweethearts, but knew each other back in grammar school.

"I went with him for two weeks in eighth grade," Barb says. "But he went with everyone in the eighth grade."

The diner, a Silk City, opened September 21, 1955. On the wall of the back dining room, the Acorn Room, is the original menu.

"It only sat forty-four people, and was one of the few air-conditioned places in South Jersey," Bob says. "That caused quite a stir."

The name was a natural—the famed five-hundred-year-old Salem Oak is right across the street.

The diner was open twenty-four hours until 1964; it is now open from 5 A.M. to 9 P.M. seven days a week.

"Everything here is original," says Bob, sitting down in a booth, where the napkins are fifties-vintage Tidy Nap dispensers. "The panels. The floors. When we need a piece of tile, we take it from underneath the booths in the Nut House . . ."

Ah, yes, the Nut House. This is the name for the alcove to the right of the counter. Anyone can sit there, but you'd better be prepared to join in the always lively conversation. A knowledge of fishing helps.

"There are still sections of South Jersey where a man's handshake means more than a piece of paper," Bob says. "And the sheer beauty of this area is unbelievable. You drive out on some of these roads in the fall and see the leaves, you won't ever have to go to New England."

Don't get the idea that he, or anyone else around here, thinks Salem County is paradise. A drawing taped to the door says, "Welcome to Salem County, where every road eventually narrows to a single lane or is detoured." It shows the county animal (a barrier horse), the county mineral (asphalt), the county flag (a stop sign), the county motto ("Single Lane Next Twenty-five Miles") and the county joke (men working).

Bob was a cook in the navy, and cooking—besides fishing, of course—is what he knows best.

"I have a reputation for fish that is unbelievable," he says. "On Friday nights during shad season, you have to take a number."

There are as many seafood dishes as meat dishes on the dinner menu. A real popular breakfast special is number 6—mackerel with fried potatoes and buttered toast.

"What makes a diner successful," Bob says, "is a good piece of liver, a good chopped steak, a good hot roast beef sandwich—your staples should be good.

"Gourmet is great to look at," he adds, "but it ain't worth shit to eat."

Bob is never at a loss for words.

"We have three cardinal rules," Barb says. "Honesty, you are not late for work, and you do not not show up for work. You do it just once and you have no job."

Barb is tougher than she looks.

All four of their sons and one daughter have worked here. One son, Steven, is a Naval Academy graduate and pilot. One day a customer walked in and complained about "some son of a bitch" who was flying over her house in a helicopter.

Waitresses at the Salem Oak dress up as elves at Christmas time. This one is Nancy Maccarone, Bob and Barb's daughter.

Jennifer Ayars, Salem Oak Diner.

"That's no son of a bitch," Barb told her. "That's my son."

The best diners have more than just good food, good atmosphere, and good help. They mean something to the community. The Salem Oak qualifies.

"We have keys to people's houses for when they go away," Bob explains. "They know we're going to be here. We let the plumber in, we know what color their house is going to be painted. We deliver prescriptions; we deliver meals. It's called diner family."

He remembers something else important to a diner's success.

"You can't change the soups. It throws people out of whack [every Tuesday at the Salem Oak, it's split pea; every Wednesday, chicken]. People go to diners on different days for different things."

Anyone famous ever eat here?

"[Margot] Kidder and Jesse Jackson, you call that famous?" he replies. "[Alleged Philadelphia mobster] Nicky Scarfo. Nicky was a good customer. He stopped by every Sunday morning after taking his mother to church. Jimmy Carter was here on a Friday

All-American dinner, Salem Oak Diner.

Behind the scenes, Salem Oak Diner.

night [when he was no longer president]. It was shad night. He came over to the diner, wanted to know why all the people were out front. He was told he had to get a ticket like everybody else."

The Salem Oak's regulars, though, are more like Marion Patrick, who stops by the diner every day and drops off roses. Her husband is buried in the cemetery across the street.

On the other hand, there have been characters aplenty here in the past forty years. Slats Plasket and Ben Haines were two of them. Slats worked in the mold shop at nearby Anchor Hocking, while Ben was a farmer. Slats lived to the age of 102, Ben well into his eighties.

"We catered [Ben's] fortieth, fiftieth, sixtieth, and sixty-fifth wedding anniversaries," Barb recalls.

Ben was in the Salem Oak one day celebrating his birthday. Slats started riding him about the "hussy in a bathing suit with no stockings" whom Ben had escorted to the beach way back in 1917. Slats was in a foul mood because Ben had forgotten *his* birthday.

Ben didn't want any hard feelings, so he left the diner and brought back a five-gallon bucket filled with manure, with a rose sticking out of it.

Slats's response: "Can you get me another five gallons of this? I want to put it in my garden."

Marlayna Masumeci, Salem Oak Diner.

An early postcard of the Burlington Diner, on Route 25 (later 130). (Courtesy of Herman Costello)

Jim's Drive In, Route 130, Windsor, 1952. (Courtesy of Jim Corcodilos)

Five Star Diner, Branchville:
a setting to match the name.

BUSINESS HOURS
Mon.-Fri. 5:00am 3:00 pm
Saturday 5:00am 2:00 pm
Sunday 5:00am 1:00 pm

250

CLOSED

The late afternoon sun fills
the Five Star's interior with
a golden light.

Eggs don't come any hotter than they do at
the Short Stop in Bloomfield. They're served
in the skillet.

The beloved Short Stop, once of Belleville, now
calls Cleveland home. Steve Harwin bought
it when the property was sold. He says he'll
never sell the little diner.

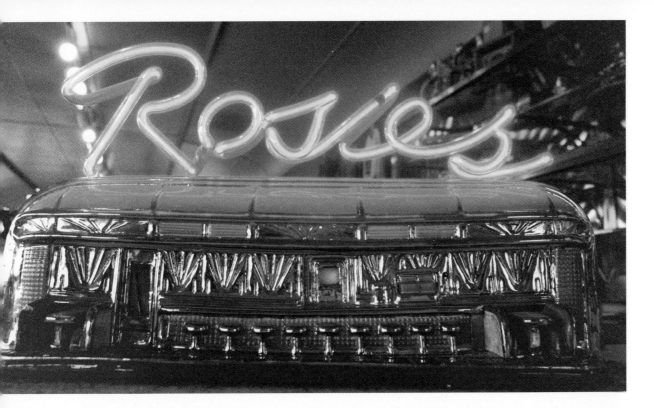

One of Jerry Berta's ceramic sculptures available for purchase at the Diner Store, next to Rosie's.

It doesn't really exist, but should: the Big Carrot Diner, one of Berta's creations.

Above, left: New Jersey's strangest-looking diner, the Luna Bell, on Route 1 in Woodbridge.

Above, right: On the other side of the railroad tracks in Paterson is Chappy's Diner, owned by Syrian immigrant Botros Astiphan.

Right: Phily Diner, Black Horse Pike, Runnemede: the only diner in the world (we hope) with a 1957 Ford Fairlane in the lobby.

The postcard-prettiest diner in the state:
The White Manna, Hackensack.

A Sodamaster drink dispenser at the White Manna.
A 1950s diner fixture, it could dispense up to
five combinations of beverages—water, soda
water, and carbonated beverages—from the
same faucet.

Glass block is one of the White Manna's
distinctive features.

The Club Diner, on the Black Horse Pike
in Bellmawr, celebrated its fiftieth anniversary
in 1996.

Take an old church bus, cover it with
stainless-steel sheathing and install some
sawed-off stools, and what've you got?
The Curbside Cafe.

The Roadside Diner in Wall, used in the John Sayles movie Baby, It's You.

Orange Circle, Orange.

KEEPING IT IN THE FAMILY

astoris on Route 130 in Bordentown is the Wal-Mart of New Jersey diners: a huge, sprawling place with a parking lot the size of many small towns and a staggering selection of items, which is why local diner owners, while wishing the Mastoris family well, of course, also wish they would just stop expanding (the capacity is now 520 people) and stop branching out into other businesses, such as outside catering.

What other diner owners and many Mastoris customers don't realize is that the family started small—real small—and that the sprawling diner on Route 130 is just the latest chapter in a remarkable family story.

◆ ◆ ◆ ♛ ◆ ◆ ◆

Mary Mastoris sits at the dining room table of her beautiful summer home; the living room windows command a breathtaking view of Barnegat Bay. It is a misty, chilly morning, a good day to sit down with a cup of coffee and look through old clippings and photographs.

"It was a tiny little place," she says of the family's first diner. "It had a little kitchen at one end."

That was the Hightstown Diner, a twelve-stool O'Mahony diner her father,

BORDENTOWN GRILL - BILL MOSKOS, PROP. — JUNCTION ROUTES 25 AND 39 - BORDENTOWN, N.J.

The Bordentown Grill was a well-known road-side attraction at the junction of Routes 25 (130) and 39 (206), where Mastoris Diner is today.

Nicholas Corcodilos, bought for seven thousand dollars in 1927. It was located on Mercer Street in Hightstown.

In his sales pitch Jerry O'Mahony did some math for Corcodilos: The average diner customer occupied his stool for eight minutes and spent twenty-five cents. The math sounded good to Corcodilos in 1927.

The diner owner had come to this country in the early 1900s. His father had been a postman, delivering mail by boat between Andros Island and Constantinople, now Istanbul. Nick Corcodilos wanted to be a cook, though, and his father found him an apprenticeship.

"He decorated food, made flowers out of vegetables," Mary Mastoris says. "He was only twelve or thirteen."

Corcodilos worked in St. Augustine, Florida, and Boston before ending up in Perth Amboy, where he ran the Presto Restaurant on State Street. He wanted to live in a town that reminded him of where he grew up in Greece—a village with trees and surrounding countryside—and found it in Hightstown.

"His dishes were better than the average lunch wagon food," Mary says of the first Hightstown Diner. "He used fresh herbs which he grew in his garden. He made his own yogurt. He would put it on top of the oven to ferment for an hour or two."

O'Mahony told Corcodilos he was doing so well that he should open another diner. He already knew a good place: Burlington. In 1929 Corcodilos opened the Burlington Diner.

There was a fellow working at the Hightstown Diner named Gus Mastoris. Gus's parents had moved to the United States from Greece but grew homesick and returned to their native country, taking their two young sons with them.

Gus and his brother, Nick, however, both born in the United States, considered themselves Americans. Gus came back first, finding a job at the Hightstown Diner. His brother followed. Nick was like a brother to Mary and her brothers, Jim and Anthony. He also worked at the Hightstown Diner. To learn English he would take the menu home at night and memorize the words.

In 1941 Mary and Nick got married.

There is a photo of Nick, Mary's father, and her brother, Anthony, standing beside Nick's Buick, parked in front of the Hightstown Diner.

"He bought that car to impress me," Mary says.

Looks like it worked.

In 1941 Nick and Mary replaced the old Hightstown Diner with a sleek, streamlined model. Two years earlier, the Burlington Diner had been replaced with a newer model.

"The men wore starched caps with their names embroidered on them," Mary says. "My stepmother made them. I remember having to iron those caps as a child. I hated that."

Every summer day she and her two brothers would peel one hundred pounds of

Why is this man smiling, and why is he sitting in a bush? Because business is good, and it's the only way that George Corcodilos, Mary Mastoris's uncle, could get himself and the Burlington Diner sign in the same shot. (Courtesy of Mary and Nick Mastoris)

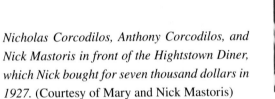

Nicholas Corcodilos, Anthony Corcodilos, and Nick Mastoris in front of the Hightstown Diner, which Nick bought for seven thousand dollars in 1927. (Courtesy of Mary and Nick Mastoris)

potatoes, "and then we could go out and play."

Nick Corcodilos sold the Burlington Diner to Nick Mastoris's brother, Gus, and several partners. After the war customers increasingly requested liquor with their meals, so Nick and Mary sold the Hightstown Diner and looked for a place with an existing liquor license, buying one from the old Bordentown Grill—a well-known roadside attraction at the junction of what were then Routes 25 and 39 (now 130 and 206). Atop the awning sat a large painted rooster.

When the Grill was torn down for a highway construction project, Nick and the owner built another diner, also called the Bordentown Grill, where Mastoris is today. It burned down in 1969; a year and a half later Mastoris opened. There were 30 employees, including 15 waitresses and 1 baker.

Today Mastoris employs 160 people, including 80 waitresses and 6 bakers. The menu lists seventy-six different sandwiches—which doesn't even include the hot sandwiches and club sandwiches—and sixteen different omelettes, including a Granny Smith omelette, with apples and cheddar cheese.

And today Nick Mastoris—along with his sons, Alex, Michael, and James, and grandson Nicholas—owns Mastoris.

And the Burlington Diner is owned by Anthony Mastoris, Nick and Mary's nephew, and a partner.

"I'll run errands if they need me," Mary says of her sons. "My husband goes in, but it's more of a social thing, to meet his friends."

Nicholas Corcodilos, one of whose favorite sayings was "Never repeat what you see or hear," died in 1974 at the age of ninety.

"He always ate well," Mary says of her father. "He always had wine at dinner. We always had salad at the table."

Jim Corcodilos inside the Country Diner on Route 130 in Windsor, which he owned for about forty years. He is now director of the First Washington State Bank.

The Hightstown Diner, Mercer Street.
(Courtesy of Mary and Nick Mastoris)

And there was always bread. The bakery is the first thing you see, and smell, as you walk into Mastoris. The bakers make cheese bread, cinnamon bread, and a sunflower-seed bread, among others.

One day a Japanese tourist who had eaten at Mastoris several days earlier stopped in with a brand-new suitcase and filled it with loaves of bread to take home.

"You should talk to my brother Jim," Mary Mastoris says, as she gathers the clippings and photos on the dining room table. "He sold his diner five months ago."

◆ ◆ ◆ ♛ ◆ ◆ ◆

"This place started in 1952," says Jim Corcodilos, sitting in a booth at the Country Diner on Route 130 in Windsor, "with a two-thousand-dollar GI loan."

But in 1952 the big craze was drive-ins, not diners. So Jim built himself a drive-in. Dug the foundation himself.

"I had blisters like you've never seen before," he recalls not so fondly.

The sign at the entrance had DRIVE IN written in white letters on a red background, and a white arrow pointing the way. CURB SERVICE, it said, and CHICKEN IN THE BASKET.

"I was the cook, dishwasher, you name it," he says. "There were only three tables. It was supposed to be open just the summer but we did so well we stayed open all year."

When companies such as McGraw-Hill and RCA started moving into the area, Jim realized that he needed more than a drive-in. He enlisted Kullman—"DeRaffele was quite backed up"—to build a diner. Jim's Country Diner opened in July 1952. The diner had big, full-length windows, characteristic of many fifties diners.

"I worked thirty-five years in a row without a day off," says Jim, a big man who wears suspenders over a plaid shirt. "I don't know if that's a record. We were closed Christmas Day, I was in here Christmas night cutting vegetables."

In 1978 he sold the diner, but he ended up buying it back a year and a half later.

"The owners didn't get along well," he recalls. "I had to separate them out in the parking lot once."

In 1994 he sold the diner again, this time for good. It is now known as the Windsor Country Diner.

He lives on a farm next to the diner, and now he's in a different line of work. In 1989 he started the First Washington State Bank. The diner man has done well as a bank director; the bank has four branches.

The diner looks much the way it did in 1952, and it still serves the best French toast in New Jersey.

And the drive-in? It's still there. The bar next door? That's it.

LOONEY BELL

H e shuffles out of the kitchen, black bushy hair escaping from under his white cap, his apron greasy, a goofy grin on his face, looking for all the world like the dishwasher, or the cleanup man, or maybe the part-time stock boy.

"You want story, come here, I give you great story," Manny Mavrorasakis had said excitedly on the phone.

Manny works at the Luna Bell on Route 1 in Woodbridge. Despite some fierce competition—diners that look like electronics stores, diners that look like mausoleums—the Luna Bell is New Jersey's strangest-looking diner.

The roof rises and falls like a bell curve. The squat chimney curves gnomishly to the right, like something out of a fairy tale. An adjoining tower—the diner vestibule—is enclosed by glass panels at the top.

It is New Jersey's only medieval-looking diner; you half expect someone to toss boiling oil from the parapet, or see knights on horseback charge across Route 1 and rescue the fair maiden imprisoned in the tower.

Judging by its looks—did I mention that the windows are porthole shaped?—the diner really should be called the Looney Bell.

"Is a little bit different," Manny confesses.

By the way, Manny's not the dishwasher, he's the owner.

Opposite: Luna Bell, Route 1, Woodbridge, once Chock Full o' Nuts.

Manny Mavrorasakis, owner and chief tour guide at the Luna Bell Diner.

A more perfect match of establishment and owner may never be found.

"People say, 'You see one diner, you've seen them all,'" he tells me. "This is not the case here."

How did the Luna Bell get its name?

"I don't know," he replies. "I think my brother." He smiles. "Is it good?"

He leads me on a tour that takes in every conceivable part of the diner, including the back of the building, where nobody goes except the dishwasher on a cigarette break.

"You can visit all the diners in the world and you will not see this," he says of the stone-embedded back wall. "It cost me twenty-five-thousand dollars. You go to all the diners, it's very nice in front and in back it's disgusting. Nobody gives a damn about the back. But everybody sees the back. I'm not saying put diamonds in the back of the goddamn thing . . ."

Everything about the Looney Bell—er, Luna Bell—is one of a kind, Manny insists.

"This is the only sign on U.S. 1 from here to Florida this high," he says of the diner's thirty-five-foot-high sign. "If you see [another] one this high, let me know."

The men's and women's restrooms, located at opposite ends of the diner?

"All diners have the same setup except this one," Manny says.

The five-thousand-pound-capacity lift that allows deliverymen to drop supplies to the cellar instead of lugging them down the stairs?

"No [other] diner has this," he says.

The rotating oven? Need you ask?

"One in one hundred diners, you will find rotating oven," he explains. "One in two hundred diners, maybe."

Throughout the interview Manny doesn't stop smiling, even when talking about his problems. He's a little hard to follow, speaking in a fast mumble that has you saying "Hmm?" every so often.

"We did the cooking downstairs in the cellar in the beginning," he says. Big smile. "Only in America."

The diner was once a Chock Full o'Nuts. Maybe not all the nuts have left.

"Listen to this," Manny says. "This is funny story."

He and his brother, George—they emigrated from Greece in 1957—were driving around one day looking for a business to buy. Their grandfather, Emanuel, had run a Texas Lunch in Hoboken. Manny and George drove past the Chock Full o'Nuts on Route 1, just north of what was then the Green Street Circle, and noticed the FOR RENT sign. The coffee shop had been closed about five years. Manny and George signed a fifteen-year lease and started to transform the shop from ugly duckling into handsome prince. Or was it the other way around?

"We took it over, broke everything," Manny recalls.

They didn't actually break anything, but they sure changed things. They tore down the horseshoe-shape counter, removed the front grill ("I tell my brother, 'You cook outside, you make it like a truck stop'"), added the kitchen, kept the steel door, added the stone facade, added the medieval-looking tower, raised the ceiling, added two dining rooms.

One Luna Bell, ready to go.

"The name [means] nothing," the fifty-eight-year-old diner owner says. "It's just identification. You could put a number out there—Number Three Diner—what does it matter?"

In these days of closed-at-midnight-or-earlier diners, the 240-seat Luna Bell remains open twenty-four hours, even if Manny sometimes has trouble finding dependable help.

"Is crazy business," he explains. "Somebody die, somebody get pregnant. I had one [waitress], her grandmother died seven times. Honest to God."

Manny's diner tour takes in the two kitchens—one for the short-order cooks, one for the chef—the cellar, where there are three huge pots filled with potatoes, and a subcellar, where the rotating oven, mixers, and other equipment are located.

"Do you know how we got this table down here?" he asks, pointing to the massive eleven-foot-long baker's table, which clearly didn't come through the door.

I try to figure it out but give up.

"We cut a hole in the ceiling and dropped it in," Manny says proudly.

Of course.

Next stop: his tornado-aftermath of an office, crammed with boxes and pieces of equipment, where his unique filing system is on display. Hundreds—no, thousands—of business cards and pieces of paper are taped every which way to the wall. On them are

The diner's sign is the tallest on Route 1 from here to Florida, according to Manny. "If you see one this high," he adds, "let me know."

Luna Bell Diner.

the names and phone numbers of suppliers, deliverymen, handymen, and others.

There is a method to the madness, naturally.

"You work on the grill, your hands are greasy," the Luna Bell's owner explains. "You don't want to open up a phone book."

Speaking of getting one's hands dirty, the waitresses in Manny's diner are not above such unwaitresslike duties as making toast, the responsibility of the kitchen help in most diners.

"What does it matter if [customers] see the girls making toast?" he asks. "This is a natural thing. This is the way they have you brainwashed in other diners. If a guy gets his food the right way, the right time, cooked the way it's supposed to be, he doesn't give a damn what you're doing back here."

The diner, he says generally, "is forever," but he admits there is increasing pressure on owners. The biggest threat to the future of diners? Chain restaurants, such as the Olive Garden and Houlihan's, he says. Ironically a developer wants to buy a piece of property Manny owns just up the road. What would be built there? An Olive Garden.

"Every business is hard business, but there is no business like this business," he says, standing in front of his distinctive tower. "This is not like shoe business. There you have to satisfy forty people a day. Here you must satisfy one thousand people a day. And you're not going to satisfy everyone.

"Crazy business," he adds. "You stay in one place, you must be crazy, too." He sticks out his hand. "Nice talking to you."

FOOD, GLORIOUS FOOD

It's late, I'm hungry, I'm tired, and all I want out of life is a cup of coffee and a menu.

The waitress drops off the menu, returns a few minutes later, and asks, "Ready to order?"

I have not made it past the first page of the menu.

Thirty-one sandwiches are listed, not counting the three open-face hot sandwiches; or the four open-face hot sandwich platters, which are different from the open-face hot sandwiches; or the eight hot sandwiches, which are different from both the open-face hot sandwich platters and the open-face hot sandwiches; or the open-face cheese steak, which features tzatziki sauce, which I later discover is eastern Mediterranean in origin, and consists of yogurt, chopped cucumbers, and garlic; or the seven club sandwiches; or the six cold subs; or the tantalizing Chicken–Cheese Steak Deluxe; or that all-time late-night diner favorite, the "pattie melt," a burger with melted cheese on rye or whole wheat bread.

I almost expect to discover "Patty Melt" listed below "Pattie Melt," and in six different versions.

All this is just the first page.

I want to ask the waitress, "Can you come back tomorrow?"

I want to ask the waitress, "Is there a large-print condensed version of this?"

The menu is eleven pages long.

If you're a regular, you can help yourself to coffee at the Dumont Crystal Diner.

Bendix Diner.

Freehold Grille.

Diner Drive-In, *February 1957.*

Is this a diner menu or a doctoral dissertation listing every food item consumed in the twentieth century?

"I have the biggest menu, I think, in the United States," says a proud James Christakos, owner of the Mays Landing Diner. He thinks about that. "It's the biggest menu in the world." Thinks again. "I do not know. I do not go everywhere."

James, let's just call it the biggest diner menu in New Jersey and leave it at that.

Wait a minute. I've just come across an equally hefty diner menu, from the Elgin Diner in Camden. It's one of those menus with all sorts of things attached; it has more supplements than the Sunday paper.

Which menu is bigger? We'll settle that issue later. First, a trip to the biggest diner in the world.

◆ ◆ ◆ ♛ ◆ ◆ ◆

"The biggest diner in the world, I used to own," Christakos is saying. "I had Glenn Miller, Harry James, all the big names before the casinos. All the big names except Frank Sinatra."

Jack Berndt, White Diamond, Elizabeth.

Pig roast, Max's Grill, Harrison.
(Courtesy of Manny Campos)

Route 4, Paramus.

Revolving cake tray, Ponzio's Brooklawn Diner.

"Lots of diners claimed to be the world's largest," I say as delicately as possible.

"A lot of them, yes, but not with one thousand seats," he replies.

He's got a point. The diner/restaurant/nightclub was the former Mediterranean, later the Bay Diner in Somers Point. Christakos owned it from 1973 to 1980.

His first business was the little Majestic Lunch in New Brunswick. Then the Terminal Diner in Jersey City. And the Princetonian Diner in West Windsor. The Toms River Diner, Crystal Diner, Galloway Diner . . . the man kept building, acquiring, and selling diners. And that included the "world's largest diner," the Bay, which somehow over the years became a furniture store.

The only diner Christakos now owns is the Mays Landing Diner, but he still owns the property where the Galloway, Toms River, and Princetonian diners are located. James Christakos is a smart guy.

The Mays Landing Diner is part old, part new, part borrowed, part . . . well, maybe not so much blue as green. Somewhere under all that stonework, marble floors, mirrors and glass chandeliers is . . .

The Tick-Tock Diner.

Summit Diner.

Time Out Diner, Tuckahoe.

Two hoagies, Time Out Diner.

Yes, the old Tick-Tock on Route 3 in Clifton, replaced by the new, $1.3 million Tick-Tock in early 1995, ended up in Mays Landing.

Old diners don't even get a chance to go to heaven.

Christakos removed the Tick-Tock's fixtures, walls, and ceiling and covered the steel frame with marble, stone, and all the rest. Added a new kitchen and dining room. Cost: about two millon dollars.

Is he done diner shopping? For the time being. Will he add on to the Mays Landing Diner? "Pretty soon," he replies.

◆ ◆ ◆ ♕ ◆ ◆ ◆

And now to the main event: Classic fifties diner (the Elgin) versus expensive new restaurantlike diner (the Mays Landing) in the Battle of the Big Menus.

Let's add up the items and see who comes out on top.

Sandwiches—Mays Landing: 65; Elgin: 83
Salads/cold platters—Mays Landing: 13; Elgin: 14
Appetizers—Mays Landing: 15; Elgin: 7
Meat and poultry dishes (including specials)—Mays Landing: 50; Elgin: 18
Pasta dishes—Mays Landing: 20; Elgin: 15
Seafood—Mays Landing: 51; Elgin: 24
Diet Delights (Mays Landing): 15; *Heart Smart Favorites* (Elgin): 14
Gourmet Greek Delights—Mays Landing: 13; Elgin: No such category
Vegetables—Mays Landing: 8; Elgin: 16
Eggs and Omelettes—Mays Landing: 26; Elgin: 28
Juices—Mays Landing: 5; Elgin: 7
Hotcakes and French Toast—Mays Landing: 10; Elgin: 9
Number of Dishes named Abu—Mays Landing: 1; Elgin: 0
Number of Dishes named Pigpen—Mays Landing: 0; Elgin: 1

Mays Landing wins eight of fourteen categories, but most were close, so we're going to a tie-breaker, which will be the most distinctive dishes, the ones you won't find anywhere else, or at least not at Denny's.

Mays Landing's nominee: "All the Way" Bagel (lox and cream cheese on a toasted jumbo bagel with lettuce, tomatoes, cucumbers, olive, radish, scallions, Bermuda onion, green pepper ring, cole slaw, and pickle).

Elgin's nominee: Egg-Lin Muffin (fried egg and American cheese with Canadian bacon, sausage, or bacon on a toasted English muffin).

And the winner is . . .

You decide. I need a few more days to get through the menus.

Five Star Diner, Branchville.

Ernie Hilling of Cresskill at the Dumont Crystal Diner.

Bendix Diner, Hasbrouck Heights.

Excellent Diner.

TEMPTING TREATS FROM DINERS AROUND NEW JERSEY:

Big Ernie's Diner: Marinated, grilled key lime chicken dinner, with soup or salad, two vegetables, rolls, and butter.

Burlington Diner: Grilled corned beef and Swiss, served on rye with french fries and cole slaw.

Court House Diner: Country omelette—with hot sausage, onions, peppers, mushrooms, and cheese.

Coach House Diner: Chili Jackets—potato skins stuffed with chili and topped with melted Monterey Jack cheese, served with nacho chips.

Luna Bell Restaurant-Diner: Turkish Beef Shish-Ke-Bab, with broiled green peppers, onions, and mushroom caps, whole broiled tomato, and Turkish pilaf.

Hammonton Diner: French Dip—fresh roast beef on a roll au jus.

Harris Diner: Black Angus steak sandwich, with lettuce, tomatoes, golden browned french-fried potatoes, and mushroom sauce.

Mastoris Diner-Restaurant: Barcelona Pizza, with roasted chicken breast, *filetto de pomodoro* sauce, artichoke hearts, feta cheese, and sun-dried tomatoes, with salad.

Miss America Diner: Greek salad—chopped green vegetables with tomatoes, feta cheese, and olives in vinegar-and-oil dressing.

Oliver's Diner: Rib sandwich with two vegetables.

Point 40 Diner: Triple-Decker Burger Surprise—beef burger, sliced minute steak, and melted Swiss cheese with sliced tomato, french-fried potatoes, and creamy cole slaw.

Reo Diner: Pancakes Luau—country sausages wrapped in pancakes with Hawaiian crushed pineapple.

Salem Oak Diner: Deviled crab cutlet with tartar sauce.

Tops Diner: Open meatloaf sandwich on hard roll with tomato sauce and topped with mozzarella cheese, served with french fries and cole slaw.

Tunnel Diner: Tunnel Burger Deluxe on a kaiser roll with melted cheese, sautéed onions, mushrooms, peppers, lettuce, tomato, french fries, and onion rings.

Westville Diner: Westville Special Melt—breast of chicken with sliced mushrooms and melted mozzarella cheese on a torpedo roll.

Wildwood Diner: Yankee pot roast with noodles and vegetable.

Clarksville Diner.

Max's Grill in Harrison, combination diner and bar, serves some of the biggest burgers anywhere.

CITY DINERS

Ladies are invited in the state's oldest diner—says so right outside the door—and inside there's a bar, which starts where the diner's Formica counter ends. "Can you get a beer for breakfast?" I ask owner Manny Campos.

"Yes," he replies. "Beer, brandy, wine. But not early in the morning. Not before seven."

Oh, well.

Max's Grill in Harrison, otherwise known as Rodas and Campos Diner Bar and Restaurant, is the oldest operating diner in the state, according to its owners.

Manny says that when he and his partner, Eduardo Rodas, bought Max's in 1989, the owners told them that the diner was eighty-three years old, which would mean it was built around 1906. That is impossible. The diner is an O'Mahony, and Jerry O'Mahony didn't start building diners until 1913.

Max's is probably the oldest diner in the state anyway; no one has stepped forward to say otherwise.

The bar keeps the diner afloat; there just isn't enough breakfast and lunch business. The prices are reasonable, though, and the burgers are huge.

"I'd like to do a lot of changes," Manny says, "but things are a little slow lately."

The previous owners, Alvaro Pinto and Armando Ferrera, owned Max's for ten years. Before that they worked in the bakery next door; they would stop in Max's for lunch. Manny was a bar owner, Eduardo a baker. When they decided to become partners, Eduardo tried to persuade Manny to buy a bakery.

Colleen Collins, White Diamond, Elizabeth.

Max's Grill in Harrison is probably the oldest diner in the state. And it's the home of Max, the house dog.

"I don't want no bakery," he recalls, smiling. "We saw this place for sale. I know the owners for long time. We came in, make sale."

He and Eduardo bought the property for $255,000.

They added new booths in the diner, TVs in the bar. The new booths look as if they belong in a pizza parlor, but they are sturdier.

A big reason Manny wanted out of the bar business was the hours. His hours at Max's are not much better. He and Eduardo each work twelve-hour shifts: 5:00 A.M.–5:00 P.M., 5:00 P.M.–5:00 A.M. Every other weekend one of them gets stuck with the fun shift: 10:30 A.M. Sunday to 5:00 A.M. Monday.

He and Eduardo, like the owners before them, are Portuguese. Someday Manny would like to leave the diner to his son, Carlos, but he started his own business, the World Cup Deli in Harrison, a year ago.

"I would like to take some time off," says Manny, fifty-one. "No week's vacation in six years."

So if you're in Newark some time, pop over the bridge into Harrison and stop at Max's. Say hello to Max, the house dog; his doghouse is out back.

Saturday's a good day for a visit. Saturday means one thing at Max's: pig roast!

◆ ◆ ◆ ♛ ◆ ◆ ◆

A diner grows in downtown Jersey City, on a stretch of road where there aren't any trees, just empty lots and the turnpike overhead.

The Newark Avenue Diner looks great now—red, white, and yellow exterior, clean as a whistle inside—but it has seen some rough times.

Back in the forties, it was known as DeKay's.

"Big grease pit," one customer recalls. "Flypaper hanging down where you ate. Big fan to suck the grease out."

Then it was a fast-food restaurant called Clem's Express, then a take-out chicken place, then Giorgio's Pizza.

"It was weird," says Pete DeSimon, who works across the street in his dad's auto body business. "One day he was open, the next day he was gone. It was good pizza."

The high point in the little diner's history came when it was used in the movie *Wise Guys.* Danny DeVito and Joe Piscopo, on the run from a mob hit, call their families from pay phones in front of the diner, repainted for the movie and renamed the Turnpike Diner.

"Get the hell out of Newark!" DeVito tells his wife.

When current owners Bob Gamache and Art Brusco bought the diner last year, it had been vacant two years.

"All the glass was broken," Bob says. "There was no counter, no equipment. Basically it was a shell. Garbage everywhere. Covered with graffiti."

The city's antigraffiti patrol took care of the spray-painted messages. The patrol goes through Jersey City, painting over graffiti with leftover paint—which accounts for the different-colored bridge trestles up the street.

Manny Campos, co-owner of Max's. He and partner Eduardo Rodas bought the diner in 1989.

The Newark Avenue Diner in Jersey City, used in the movie Wise Guys, *in which it was called the Turnpike Diner.*

The little diner does a brisk breakfast business. Rod "Junior" Gamache, Bob's brother, says the potato salad is "world famous, or soon will be."

Like city diners everywhere, the Newark Avenue Diner serves the basics—eggs, burgers, fries, and the like—to its largely blue-collar clientele. You won't find anything with tzatziki sauce at any of these places.

A teenage kid on roller blades steps inside the door.

"No roller blades inside," Junior says.

"But I'm inside already," the kid protests.

"You're going out."

Bob would like to put tables and chairs outside. It would not be the most scenic lunch spot—there's a big, weed-covered lot next door and the turnpike overhead—but a welcome touch for this stretch of Newark Avenue.

"All in all," Bob says, surveying his diner, "it's working pretty good."

◆ ◆ ◆ 👑 ◆ ◆ ◆

The tired look on Botros Astiphan's face says, This business is killing me.

The tired look on Botros Astiphan's face says, If someone offered me a decent price for this diner, I would be out of here in a second.

But he has his two children, Lilian and Badr, to think of. This is why he and his wife, Samira, work in Chappy's Diner, in Paterson, from 5:00 A.M. to 4:30 P.M. every day.

"I don't work for myself," he says, "I work for them. I hope they make it."

He bought Chappy's ten years ago. The 1950s Silk City diner is named for original

White Diamond, Elizabeth.

Route 1, Jersey City.

owner Chappy DeGrazia. The diner sits in a forlorn area of Paterson, literally on the other side of the railroad tracks. The sign reads CHAPPY'S DINEP—Botros doesn't have the money to fix the *R*—and next to it is a yellow sign that says PIZZA, which Botros doesn't make anymore: not enough demand.

"I came to this country, 1982," the Syrian diner owner says. "I worked here and there. My destiny drove me here. I was looking for real estate. Somebody said, can you do it?" He smiles. "Anything you put in front of me, I can do."

Chappy's may be the bluest diner in New Jersey; the exterior is two-tone blue, the booths a deep blue, light blue curtains. There are two counters, with eight stools on each side. The jukeboxes at each booth don't work; they're not worth fixing, Botros says.

"If you change this diner, what you want to change?" he asks. "I like it the way it is. I could build an addition but first I like the place full. Why should I build an addition if the place is not full?"

He goes into the kitchen and returns with two plates of ravioli for his children, who stop in after school. Lilian promptly dips her sleeve in her plate.

"That building over there, Sealy Mattress," says Botros, pointing to an abandoned factory across the tracks. "They had three hundred people working there. Then they moved. This area was hit badly in the recession, depression, whatever you want to call it."

The look on his face says, There must be a better way to make a living.

"You have to work a lot to generate money. A hundred customers buy a cup of coffee, that's sixty dollars."

Has he taken a vacation lately?

"Vacation?" he smiles. "We don't have that benefit. Only vacation: Christmas, Thanksgiving, Memorial Day, holidays. Maybe vacation five years from now.

"Really, I should stop," he says later, leaning on the counter as if for support. "Too tiring."

◆ ◆ ◆ ♕ ◆ ◆ ◆

Market Tower, Market Street, Newark.

The former Mack Diner on French Street in New Brunswick is now All Ears Records.

*Jacqueline and Gwen Oliver flank their mom,
Corene, cook and co-owner of Oliver's Diner in
Trenton, where you can get not-so-ordinary
diner food like sweet potato pie.*

The diner floats like a mirage in the oppressive midsummer heat, a stainless steel vision in a neighborhood of abandoned factories and rundown houses on the east side of Trenton.

There is just one car in the parking lot this morning. Maybe that shouldn't come as a surprise; East State Street, or at least this part of it, has been a road to nowhere since the factories closed.

The diner's vestibule is as hot as an oven; you hesitate at the door, wondering if the place has air-conditioning.

You hesitate at the door, wondering if the diner is rundown and decrepit, like the neighborhood.

One step inside, and you're not sure if the diner's open, because nobody seems to be around. Blinds filter out the searing light outside. The soft blue walls and ceiling have a calming effect. A jungle of plants sprouts from a table at one end; letters, folders, magazines, phone books, and a Tiffany lamp are crammed into a booth. A talk-show host blabs on a nearby TV. Cardboard boxes are piled on the floor; a computer in the corner is covered with a garbage bag.

Is this a diner, you wonder, or someone's living room?

"Welcome," Gwen Oliver says in her soft, lilting voice.

Welcome to Oliver's Diner, owned by Gwen's mom, Corene, where the four-page menu is fitted inside a plain binder, where two eggs, toast, and grits or home fries will cost less than two dollars, where you can get not-so-ordinary diner fare like sweet potato pie and dilly bread.

Oliver's—Mountain View No. 318, at this location for almost twenty years—is owned by Corene and her husband, who is quick to remind everyone that he is pretty damn perfect.

Corene's husband is *named* Perfect. That's his real name. From birth.

"He had the unmitigated gall to give my brother the same name, and he was an ugly baby," Jacqueline Oliver says of her father.

She and Gwen are twins. Both are diabetics.

"This is the last place I should be in," Jackie says, laughing.

She and her sister grew up army brats, following their father from base to base. Fort Carson, Colorado, where Gwen and her sister were born; Granite City, Illinois; Fort Leonard Wood, Missouri; Indian Head, Maryland; Fort Benning, Georgia; Schilling Manor, Kansas; Fort Ord, California; New Jersey's own Fort Dix. Okinawa, even. Perfect Oliver also did two tours in Vietnam.

The family moved to Mount Holly in the seventies.

"The first four months, I expected to see a moving van come up the street," Gwen says, laughing.

When Perfect retired, he and his wife searched for a business to buy. They looked around Camden, didn't like what they saw. One day they happened to drive by the diner on East State Street.

Twenty years ago the diner was a busy place. Twenty years ago the neighborhood was a prosperous one.

"DeLaval, Switlik, Hamilton Rubber, Bayer Aspirin . . . ," says Gwen, ticking off the businesses once located here. "We had twenty-six different truck companies—not truck drivers—coming by every day."

"Lunchtime you couldn't get in here," Corene says.

But about ten years ago the factories started closing down, and business at Oliver's

Harrison Avenue, Harrison.

Capitol Lunch, Broad Street, Newark.

Bottom, left: Vassilios Venizelos,
Miss America Diner.

Bottom, right: Miss America Diner, Jersey City.

began an inexorable downward slide. Union Camp is still open but it's largely automated. Switlik, once a renowned parachute maker, no longer makes parachutes, although it does make life vests and life rafts.

Somehow the diner manages, through the perseverance of three strong women. Corene does all the cooking. Gwen, the waitress, calls her "ma'am." Jackie calls her "boss."

"My mother's a great cook," Jackie says. "She makes a mean sweet potato pie. . . ."

"Spareribs that melt in your mouth," Gwen adds.

"A real southern peach cobbler, and cornbread that's sweet, not hard like some southern cornbreads are," Jackie says.

Dilly bread? Bread whose not-so-secret ingredients are dill seed, butter, and spices.

"Whenever she gets the muse, she goes off on all different kinds of tangents," Jackie says. "She could get you to eat shredded cardboard."

The stainless-steel pans up front are filled not with sauces and gravies but with baby pictures, Philadelphia Phillies souvenirs, and more envelopes and bills. One clock says 11:30, another 10:45.

"My life," says a guest on the talk show, "was a living hell."

For atmosphere Mr. Perfect's diner is hard to beat.

But if you want to enjoy it, get down to East State Street soon, because it sounds as if the three women in Mr. Perfect's life might be ready to move on to another business.

"It's really slow," Gwen said in her singsong voice. "He's made it eighteen years. I don't know if I want to make it to nineteen."

Harrison Avenue, Harrison.

Liberty Diner, North Brunswick.

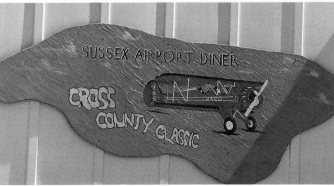

Now Tina's Kountry Kitchen, Route 639, Wantage, Sussex County.

Uniform, White Diamond, Elizabeth.

The former White Diamond, later Samantha's, in Westfield, now (sob!) the office of a Chevrolet dealership.

Two hungry customers at the White Diamond, Elizabeth.

THE DINER QUEEN AND OTHER FANATICS

They sat in three of their favorite diners—the once-married, now-separated couple who spent much of their youth in diners; the "semi-half-assed retired" salesman whose diner scrapbook has made the rounds of dozens of diners in North Jersey; and the Diner Queen herself, who earned her name the night she walked into a North Bergen diner with yellow-, pink-, and green-spiked hair, a leopard-print top, and sunglasses—and proceeded to sing "Girls Just Want to Have Fun."

"It's a typical Marion thing," the Diner Queen is saying. "If I am not happy where I am, I'll just say, 'I'll be back, I'm not going far,' and I'll just go to the diner. I'll get what I want, I'll get my turkey sandwich, I'll get my French toast."

"As a photographer a lot of the excitement is the approach to the diner," Christine Guedon-DeConcini explains. "You're going there at two in the morning, going up this hill and there's darkness, and you see this flash of pink-and-orange neon . . . you really get turned on by it."

"You can go to a diner," Ken Parker says, "and not feel self-conscious—'Does my jacket match my shoes?'"

"When you've got a trucker that lives in Boston and makes a run to Baltimore and he stops somewhere near Trenton and he sits in a diner, he knows the people in the diner and he's closer to them than he is his own neighbors back home," Steve Lintner says.

They come from different backgrounds and express themselves in different ways, but these four people share one belief—the world would be a much poorer place without diners.

"When you're out as much as I am," Marion Machucici says, "you have to know where the diners are."

Friends call her the Diner Queen, and for good reason. Name any diner within thirty miles of North Bergen and she's been there. Maybe even sung there, too.

"When I come to a diner, I feel like I'm getting something for my money," Marion says, sitting in a booth at the Coach House Diner in North Bergen. "Those are the values I was brought up with."

In front of her was a plate of French toast. This wouldn't be unusual except that it was 8 P.M.

"There is never a wrong time for French toast," she explains.

Her parents, from Jersey City, allowed Marion and her brother to choose where they wanted to have their family birthday celebrations.

"Being the kind of girl who wanted to please everyone, I usually picked a place where my parents could get a drink, where I could get dressed up, and where my skinny little brother could eat his beloved spaghetti and meatballs."

A diner.

Her favorite childhood hangout was Tippy's Charcoal Haven on Kennedy Boulevard in Jersey City. Tippy's wasn't so much diner as drive-in, and a great one. It was not a happy day in the Machucici household when Marion's mom discovered that her daughter had been skipping Sunday mass to hang out at Tippy's.

"High school, we were big at the VIP Diner [in Jersey City]," Marion says. "It was on the way back from Saint Dominic's Academy. On senior prom night, after a night in Manhattan, we all headed to the Coach House.

"It was sort of a magical place for me, a safe haven," she says of the Coach House. I still love the place; I went there prior to some minor surgery last year, just for good luck."

Last year, for her birthday, Marion and three friends went on a one-day diner blitz.

First stop, for breakfast: the Park Diner in Montclair, with its distinctive sliding bathroom door. Marion, not surprisingly, had French toast. Then came the Harris Diner in East Orange, where the four split a Sputnik, the diner's famed open-face beef sandwich. By mid-afternoon, they found themselves at Max's Grill in Harrison.

"All the boys are at Max's drinking beer and shooting pool," she says of the bar's largely male, and Portuguese, clientele. "In walk four women." She laughs. "It was an out-of-body experience."

"When you're out as much as I am," explains Marion Machucici, "you have to know where the diners are."

"You meet the damndest people in diners,"
Ken Parker says, laughing.

They had a great time.

On the way home they visited the Short Stop in Bloomfield, where they had coffee, and the White Circle System, also in Bloomfield, where they shared a couple of burgers and shakes.

Her three friends, who thought the birthday girl was carrying this diner thing too far, now share her enthusiasm.

"They're my spotters," says Marion, a manager of market resources for CBS Marketing. "They are constantly on the lookout for diners for me. It's 'Have you seen this place, have you seen that place?'"

Whenever she'd go down the shore, she'd stop at the Ocean Bay Diner in Point Pleasant. One day she discovered to her horror that her beloved "OB" had been renovated.

"I went in there—I'm screaming, 'What have they done? Oh, my God!' All these people are looking at me—what is wrong with this girl?" She laughs. "I squeak on a regular basis, but I was really squeaking then."

She got over it. "You've got to forgive and forget. You have a tantrum and let go. That's what life's all about, right?"

◆ ◆ ◆ 👑 ◆ ◆ ◆

"There's a guy who goes around taking pictures of diners you should talk to," several diner owners told me while I was researching this book.

That guy is Ken Parker, the semi-half-assed retired one.

Five years ago two pivotal events took place. Rosie's Diner ("I had a million cups of coffee in that place") was shipped to Michigan, and Tommy's Diner in Wallington burned down.

"My God," Ken thought at the time, "these things are disappearing."

He leaned back in a booth at the Summit Diner, his favorite Jersey diner. Ken, born in Summit, lives in Florham Park. While we were at the Summit Diner, he ran into someone he hadn't seen in twenty years.

"We met the goddamnedest people," Ken says of the diner excursions he and his wife would take. At one diner they met a guy who looked like "an old outlaw biker . . .

Front Street, Plainfield.

three hundred pounds on the hoof, right out of Central Casting, with 'Mama' tattooed on his back."

Ken took out his scrapbook and "before you knew it, everyone in the place was gabbing about diners."

The former packing systems salesman became friends with painter John Baeder, who depends on Ken for New Jersey images. In his book *Diners* (Harry N. Abrams, 1995), Baeder returned the favor.

In the window of Baeder's painting of the White Rose System in Linden, sand-wiched between a row of American flags and a sign that says "Fish Fryday Special," is a poster that says, "New Jersey Diners Photographs by Ken Parker."

"I don't think I've been this thrilled since my kids were born," he says.

Ken, who makes reproduction furniture, has this dream. He wants to build a scaled-down diner in his basement.

"A little six-seater," he says.

◆ ◆ ◆ 👑 ◆ ◆ ◆

"The couple find diner architecture a harmonious blend of function and bygone fashion," the newspaper story said. "In general, the couple view diners as havens of constancy and individuality in a fast-paced overly homogenized world."

Fortunately Christine Guedon-DeConcini and Steven Lintner don't talk like that.

"Going to a diner is almost like stopping at Grandma's house to get cookies and milk when your parents really don't know where you are," says Steve, sitting in the Elgin Diner.

They attended Haddon Township High School but discovered well before that how warm and inviting diners could be.

"When I was seven or eight, my mom would take me to Yvonne's," Christine says of a former diner in Westmont. "I'd say, 'Let's go to the blue place.'"

"In Haddon a diner was a place where junior high and high school students were allowed to go after hours," Steve explains. "The diner was a safe place. You're not going to some unknown friend's house where there might be some illicit activity going on."

In high school they'd go to the Diamond Diner in Cherry Hill, located next to the late great Latin Casino. The show inside the diner was as good as any inside the nightclub: the conversation, the arguments, the elderly women furtively slipping spoons into their handbags.

But their favorite observation post was a corner booth at the Oaklyn Diner. They sat on pink seats; behind them, in the rounded glass corner window, everything appeared distorted. The world was a funhouse, and they had the best seats.

They married and lived in California for several years; when they returned, they drove past the Oaklyn Diner and were shocked. It had been converted into a "stone box." Gone was the curved glass corner, gone was the pink neon lighting. It was as if their own home had been vandalized.

"Diners," says Christine Guedon-DeConcini, shown here in front of a roadside eatery in Maine, *"are as eternal as a cup of coffee."*

They decided it was their mission to "save" diners, and started collecting old diner menus, matchbooks, and photos.

When he was seventeen, sitting in the Oaklyn Diner, Steve thought about writing a nationwide diner guide. He says it's "still very much a desire and a dream," but Christine, a freelance photographer, may beat him to it. The one-time diner waitress (at the American Diner in Philadelphia) hopes to publish a "down-home, everybody's diner guide" to the country's one hundred best vintage diners.

They now live separate lives, but their love for diners is stronger than ever.

Route 9 at Route 83, Claremont.

Geet's Diner, Black Horse Pike, Williamstown.

"They're not elite establishments; they're everyday, common," says Steve, a vintage car restorer. "And they've survived in the face of the onslaught [on the commercial landscape]."

What's ugly when it comes to diners?

"Seashells on the side," Christine says, laughing.

"Something absolutely characterless," Steve says.

Taking her cue from the old Jerry O'Mahony slogan, "In our line we lead the world," Christine says that in New Jersey the line should be, "In our decline we lead the world."

But even she can appreciate New Jersey's odder-looking diners. She calls Ponzio's Brooklawn Diner a "mausoleum," but she'd rather have Ponzio's than a diner that's been "stuccoed over."

Steve strikes up a conversation with a man sitting behind us. The man talks about his recent bypass surgery; Steve tells him that George Vallianos, the Elgin's owner, will take care of any special dietary needs. The man calls himself "the best real estate agent in the state of New Jersey," and tries to sign Steve up in the business.

"These things don't happen in a Denny's," Steve says after the man leaves. "They don't happen in a restaurant where all the tables are separated by banquettes and plants."

At a Society for Commercial Archeology Pennsylvania/South Jersey diner conference in 1993, Christine described a diner's appeal:

"A place where you're called by your first name, a place where you can poke fun at the grill cook, where you can give a waitress a ride, where you'll take fresh flowers from your garden.

"America is spending. America is losing ground. America is insecure. Although they are threatened, diners are as eternal as a cup of coffee. They provide a sanctuary for those who need a brief escape. We can go alone and sit at the counter. We can go with friends and family. Someone will be telling a story. Someone else will be inspired to chime in. Diners are human. Diners are truth and beauty."

Ray Ness, Colonial Diner, Lyndhurst.

THE DINER FANATICS' FAVORITE DINERS:

Marion:

Best overall: The Coach House, North Bergen. "A neighborhood place. The coffee and the French toast are very good. Delicious mini corn muffins on the salad bar."

Best small diner: Lucy's, Verona. "Portions are enormous, people are friendly; it's like sitting down at a big Italian family dinner."

Best French toast: The Waterfalls, Ridgefield. "Instead of the regular challah bread, they use long pieces of thick bread."

Best-looking vintage diner: The Harris Diner, East Orange. "It's so immaculate and well-kept, you just feel like you could eat off the floors. I like that there's a jukebox at every booth."

Most unusual diner bathroom: The Park Diner, Montclair. "At the far end of this diner, there's a sliding door. Then you walk up two steps to the one toilet in the place."

Best omelette: The Summit Diner, Summit. "The bacon, ham, and cheese omelette is huge, packed full of bacon, with slices of real ham on top, and the cheese is so perfectly melted."

Friendliest owner and best highway diner: The Bendix Diner, Hasbrouck Heights. "When I was at the Bendix with a friend, Tony, the owner, showed us all the photos of the original place, and the snapshots of him with Whoopi Goldberg and the cast of *Boys on the Side.* Tony told me, 'Next time there's a movie here, I'll call you. I'll tell them you're my niece.'"

Best Jersey Shore diner: The Ocean Bay, Point Pleasant. "The waitresses are a little sassy, but the service is still very good. I wouldn't think of getting my French toast at any other place down the shore!"

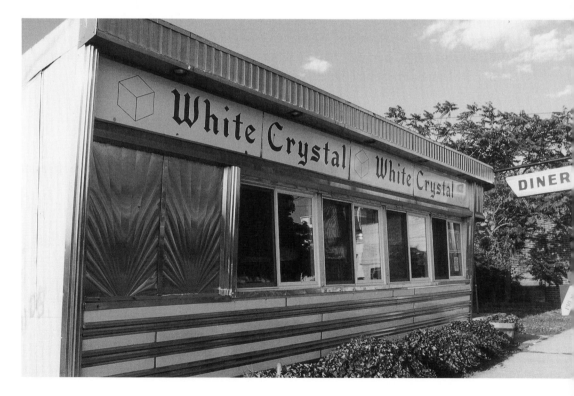

White Crystal, Atlantic Highlands.

Ken:

Bendix Diner: "Friendly people, great hash browns, especially if you ask for extra onions."

Bound Brook Diner: "It's all original. And the waitresses are real diner waitresses."

Chappy's Diner: "Nice family atmosphere. Lot of times you go there, the [owner's] kids are studying."

Five Star Diner: "A beautiful place. Last time we stopped there, it was closed, and the whole [Heater] family was out there, working in the garden."

Andover Diner: "It's been done over a few times but the interior is great. The food— good all-around American food—is outstanding."

Harris Diner: "Try the Hobo Eggs. It's kind of like a Western omelette, with bits of ham, onions, salami, peppers, eggs, potatoes, all chopped up together."

Roadside Diner: "I just love that red and yellow [color scheme]. Great cheese-burgers."

Summit Diner: "My first diner ever. They got these big-assed Boston butt hams, just gorgeous hams. And that black marble counter . . ."

Teamster's Diner: "It's really funky. It's one of those diners that should be in a part of town where all the drunks hang out."

Tom's Diner: "An original. You go in there, they include you in the conversation. You have to have a sense of humor."

Christine:

Angie's Bridgeton Grill: "You sit inside, it's really nice on a summer afternoon with the windows open and the river behind it. They have this tiny bathroom like on a train or something."

Angelo's Glassboro Diner: "Very much a community diner for many years. Friendly, comfortable place. Still has the grill out front so you can see your food being cooked."

Salem Oak Diner: "Great neon oak-leaf sign in front of the diner. The goofiness of the Acorn Room, and the Nut House."

Summit Diner: "One of the only ones in New Jersey with the marble counter left."

White Manna: "Because it's novel as far as the structure."

Barnegat Light.

Teamster's Diner: "It's sitting there on that big parking lot all by itself. The owner was not really that friendly. He did not think highly of diner lovers."

Elgin Diner: "Does a really good job at keeping up the family tradition. Very immaculate. The food is really good there."

Harris Diner: "One example of the L-shaped O'Mahony. Kind of a cool-looking place."

Summit Diner.

HOW TO DECORATE YOUR DINER

As far as I can tell, there are two basic ways to decorate a diner:

1. Find as many faded snapshots of Mom and Pop and autographed photos of extremely minor celebrities as you can and tape them to the walls.
2. Spend several million dollars on fancy neon, ornate entrances, marble statues, and the like.

Let's visit two diners to see how each decorating method is put into practice.

◆ ◆ ◆ ♛ ◆ ◆ ◆

This is all you need to know about the kind of people whose photos grace the wall at the Dumont Crystal Diner:

Annie Oakley is next to Sitting Bull—okay, we get that—and on the other side of Annie Oakley is . . . Dolly Parton?

Farther down there are photos of John Wayne, JFK—and Burt Reynolds.

And hanging in a corner is Norman Rockwell's famous painting of the runaway boy sitting on a diner stool next to the town cop.

Every diner in New Jersey, it seems, has a copy of that Norman Rockwell painting. If it's not actually hanging, it's in the basement, in the owner's attic—somewhere.

Time Out Diner, Tuckahoe.

Dumont Crystal Diner.

Actually the Dumont, built in the 1920s, has more than just mom-and-pop pictures. There are photos from the forties and fifties in a display case next to the menu boards. In one of the photos you can see the original diner.

Today the Dumont Crystal is unremarkable from the outside—the barrel roof seems swallowed up by the sign and shrubbery, but the interior is wonderful, like somebody's den, with trophies and photos and posters and stuff everywhere.

No wonder movie scouts love the place.

"Woody Allen wants to make movie here but I don't want him to make it," owner Momir Saranovic says. "He wants to change things around. I don't like the idea. I like to keep it the same."

Roney's, Route 130, Pennsauken.

The Roadside Diner, Wall.

An unlikely sight in downtown Decorah, Iowa: the Clarksville Diner, once on Route 1 in Lawrence, near what is now Quaker Bridge Mall.

The Brooklawn (formerly the South Grove) Diner, Route 130 South.

The Elgin Diner, on Mount Ephraim
Avenue in Camden, opened as the Fair-Lynne
Diner in 1958.

Gemini Diner, Route 206, Newton.

White Crown, Linden.

Pastry case, Phily Diner.

Salem Oak Diner.

Miss America Diner,
West Side Avenue,
Jersey City.

Route 40, Black Horse Pike, Pleasantville.

Salem Oak Diner.

The Chatham Wok Diner went from Chinese to Mexican, but its diner soul remained.

Route 130, Pennsauken.

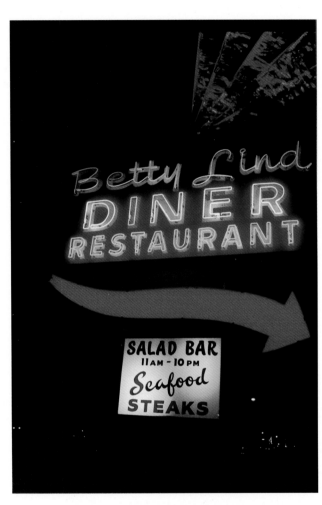

St. Georges Avenue (Route 27), Linden.

Mount Laurel Diner, Route 73.

Excellent Diner, Westfield.

Bound Brook Diner.

54 Diner, Route 54, Buena.

54 Diner, Buena.

The Rainbow Diner, Route 70, Brick.

Why are pictures of Dolly Parton, Annie Oakley, and Sitting Bull on the Dumont Crystal's walls? Who knows—maybe they ate here once.

Old photos above the counter, celebrity pictures on the wall, and things hanging from the ceiling: Few diners are as homey as the Dumont Crystal.

Old-fashioned, almost Victorian, in atmosphere, the Dumont Crystal has been coveted by filmmakers. Woody Allen reportedly wanted to use the diner in a movie, but owner Momir Saranovic said no.

Some college kids were in here last year shooting a movie. They didn't want to change things around, so Momir—"Mo" to everyone here—let them use the diner.

What was their movie about? Jack Kevorkian.

As far as I know, there is no connection between diners and "Doctor Death."

"Everybody talks about America, how it's a big thing," says Mo, who emigrated from the former Yugoslavia when he was twenty-three. "I took a big chance. I am glad I did."

He worked at several local restaurants, including the Showcase in Cresskill. One day the Crystal's owner stopped in the Showcase and asked Mo if he wanted to buy a diner.

"I don't know this place at all," he recalls. "I saw it and said, Let me take a chance. And I am glad I did. You have to take a chance in your life."

Asked how the diner was doing when he bought it twenty years ago, Mo pushes his hands toward the ground.

"Now it is steady," he says. "The first thing I did, we clean up. All new dishes, all new supplies. It took us two, three years for the business to come up."

Did he have any partners?

"No," he says, smiling. "My wife."

Dragica Saranovic can be found at the register every day.

Mo's here at 4:15 every morning "to make grill, make coffee, make everything going," he says. The diner opens at 5:00 A.M.

It's a blue-collar crowd, and they pay blue-collar prices. Two eggs with bacon, sausage, or ham, and coffee: $2.35; Pancakes: $1.75.

The specials never change. If it's Monday, it must be spaghetti and meatballs, and meatloaf; Tuesday, pot roast; Wednesday, corned beef and cabbage; Thursday, fresh turkey with stuffing; Friday, linguine with clam sauce, and a fish.

Regular Tim King has been thrown out of the diner every day for years, and keeps promising he'll never come back, but he does, and Mo lets him. These two spend most of the time insulting each other. It's all part of an act.

"So say something nice about the diner," I tell King.

He looks at his cup of coffee and says, "So what kind of oil do you use in your car?"

A gleaming bubble-tube jukebox fits right in amid the neon splendor of the Phily Diner.

◆ ◆ ◆ ♛ ◆ ◆ ◆

Ninety miles and a million dollars away from the Dumont Crystal is a diner that outglitters every other diner in New Jersey, which is not an easy thing to do.

"This is our first diner," says John Balis, sitting amid the neon-lit splendor of the Phily Diner on the Black Horse Pike in Runnemede. "First we start New Jersey, then we go Pennsylvania, then we go to Florida."

The Tick-Tock Diner in Clifton approaches the Phily in its expensive retro-fifties look, but the Tick-Tock doesn't have a lobby like the Phily's.

The brightly lit space is glass-blocked, mirrored, and stocked with the usual diner lobby features—phones, framed photos, cigarette machine. But there's something else—a gleaming 1957 Ford Fairlane.

You're not sure whether you're walking into a diner or a nightclub.

The Tick-Tock Diner, on Route 3, Clifton, was modernized in early 1995, but the old sign and clock, fortunately, remained.

Pie case, Phily Diner, Runnemede.

"Lots of cars for sale," the forty-year-old Balis says. "You can find cars anywhere."

You can find fishing boats anywhere, too. Doesn't mean you're going to put one in your lobby just because you own a seafood restaurant.

But from the beginning, John and his partners—Peter Balis, John Balis, and Petro Kontos—decided they were going to give South Jersey a diner unlike any it had ever seen.

Outside, the mirror-finish stainless-steel facade shimmers in the sun. Inside, multicolored neon races across the ceiling like something at the entrance to a futuristic amusement park ride. Fat tubes flanked by yellow lights cover the ceiling in the side dining room. Some customers, mostly of the male variety, do not notice all this at first, entranced by the young waitresses in short, tight black skirts.

This is diner as Broadway show, and we're not talking matinee.

People who were fond of the old Century Diner may keel over when they discover that this is the same place.

Several diner owners in the area laughed when asked their opinion of the Phily, but John understands as much as they do a diner's appeal.

"I think the history of America is the diner," he says. "Not seafood restaurant, not fast food. Diner. Good food, low prices."

The modern look: Great Falls Diner, Route 46, Little Falls.

The interior was conceived by Florham Park–based restaurant designer Francesco "Frank" Conte, a former designer for Musi and Fodero who has worked on more than 350 diners.

"I'm Italian; I get along with the Greeks," Conte says. "Maybe because I'm not Greek, they trust me."

All the glitz and glitter come at a price, of course. Two eggs and bacon here cost $5.50. The food may cost more, but it sure sounds good. How about a Waffle Jubilee—malted waffle with rich, creamy vanilla ice cream and hot sweet cherries in a brandy sauce?

"I own a restaurant like a diner [the Adelphia Restaurant in Deptford], but I never do a diner before," says John, sitting at a table littered with papers, an attaché case, and a cellular phone.

The group's next venture will be the Adelphia Diner in Huntington Valley, Pennsylvania, which will be a "diner diner," John says.

"It's going to be like 1940s," he explains.

The Phily's co-owner asks about this book, and he immediately turns into marketing wizard.

"You'll be able to sell one hundred thousand books," he says. "Send one hundred books to one thousand diners. No, two million—you get two million Greeks, everyone buys one." He smiles. "I guarantee you five hundred thousand."

I'm not sure if this guy should be working for Madison Avenue or K-Tel Records.

Where will his next Jersey diner be located?

"I'm looking all over to buy. Whatever comes first."

He walks over to the cash register, talks to someone on the phone, and returns to the table.

"America is diner," he says. "That's what America is about. Everything else is bullshit."

AT THE SIGN OF THE SCOTTY DOG

In a decade of nutty advertising, wacky promotions, and eye-catching displays, the diner on Route 17 in Mahwah managed to stand out.

By day it was a traffic-stopping sight, as motorists craned their necks out their windows to make sure they were seeing right.

By night the forty-foot-high tower glowed as if it were on fire; the restaurant's name was lit up. THE TOWER OF PIZZA. Part diner, part drive-in, part pizza parlor. "Patience and pizza have paid off in towering success for Michael and John Manna," according to a 1957 article in *Diner Drive-In* magazine.

The two Jersey City brothers had turned in their uniforms for pastrymen's hats after World War II. Five years of "patient thought and investigation" resulted in the idea of an Italian restaurant with a gimmick—a tower patterned after the Leaning Tower of Pisa. The porcelainized steel Tower of Pizza leaned, too.

Inside the Paramount diner, there was room for forty-eight people at fourteen stools and eight tables. The adjoining patio seated another fifty people under brightly colored translucent Fiberglas canopies. The two-acre parking lot could hold three hundred cars.

But what many customers remembered, more than the food, maybe even more than the tower, were the caps: All Tower of Pizza employees wore a white beret topped with a pasteboard tower; they looked like extras in some loopy 1950s sci-fi movie.

That same 1957 issue of *Diner Drive-In* carried a story about the menu at the

Route 23, Franklin, Sussex County.

The Tower of Pizza, a traffic-stopping sight on Route 17, Mahwah, in the 1950s. The forty-foot-high porcelainized steel tower leaned just like the rhyming Tower of Pisa. (Courtesy of Herb Enyart)

Totem Drive-In in Royal Oak, Michigan. You could order a Shawnee ("Delicious Fried Chicken Savage Style . . . For Easy Eatum With Fingers"), a Mohawk ("Heap Good Spare Ribs With Little Squaws Special Bar-B-Q Sauce"), or the Iroquois ("Fan Tail Gulf Shrimp With Snappy Camp Fire Sauce"). And, for dessert, Strawberry Short Cake with Ice Cream Tepee Style.

The Tower of Pizza, fortunately, didn't have to resort to such silliness. Its menu, shaped like the tower itself, included the Tower of Pizza Burger ($.50 in 1957), Charcoal Broiled Steak with french fries and salad ($2.95), and 21 Shrimp in Basket ($1.25).

◆ ◆ ◆  ◆ ◆ ◆

White Tower, Camden. (Courtesy of White Tower Corporation)

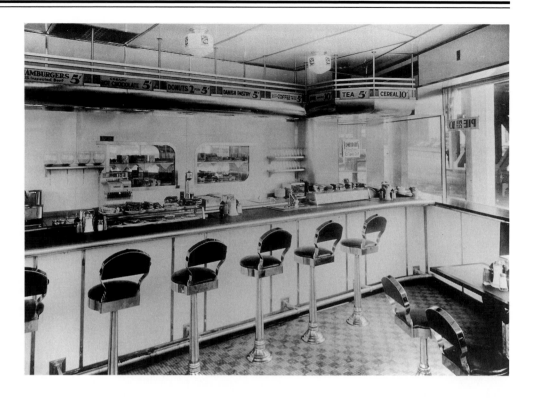

White Tower, Paterson. (Courtesy
of White Tower Corporation)

White Tower, Red Tower, Blue Castle, White Castle, White Top, White Jay, White
Diamond, White Star . . . these were the twelve-stool-or-less twenty-four-hour hamburger joints that first sprang up in 1921, with the opening of a White Castle in Wichita,
Kansas. In 1926 the first White Tower opened in Milwaukee, Wisconsin, and by 1935
there were more than 130 White Towers from Boston to Minneapolis.

White Towers were glistening white buildings with a tower atop one corner; white
was chosen because it evoked cleanliness and wholesomeness.

The tower, according to Paul Hirshorn and Steve Izenour, authors of the evocative
White Towers (MIT Press, 1979), mirrored the 1920s taste in exotic architectural
themes; movie theaters of the time displayed Moorish, Egyptian, or Mayan influences.

The towers were meant to suggest "a severely stripped version of a medieval fortress but packaged in a bold shape and clad in white glazed brick," write Hirshorn and Izenour.

In the beginning hamburgers weighed one ounce, were served on a two-inch-diameter roll, and cost five cents. Everything was served on paper napkins.

By the mid-1950s, there were 230 White Towers across the country.

"The best stuff they did [architecturally] was in New Jersey," says Izenour, an associate with the architectural firm Venturi Scott Brown and Associates in Philadelphia.

A White Tower that once stood on the White Horse Pike in Camden, he says, was "the most gorgeous one of all time."

◆ ◆ ◆ 👑 ◆ ◆ ◆

"That pigeon we have stationed in Trenton, N.J.," read the news item in the June 1947 issue of *The Diner,* "just flew in with raves about Fritz Plassmeyer's new diner and his delicious coffee."

A year later the "pigeon" brought this news: "Tremendously successful, Fritz has acquired a store of knowledge probably second to none."

Who was Fritz Plassmeyer, and why were people saying wonderful things about him?

He was the German-born owner of Fritz's Diner on Calhoun Street in Trenton, one of the busiest diners in the state at the time. Fritz had been an apprentice blacksmith in Bremen, then a butcher, and by the time he reached the United States, what he wanted to do more than anything was cook.

In 1930 he and a friend, Al Buettemuller, bought a run-down, bankrupt diner on Brunswick Avenue in Trenton for $2,500. It did so well that they bought a second, on Calhoun Street. The two dissolved their partnership, and Fritz ended up owning the latter operation, a barrel-roofed diner in an industrial area. In five years Fritz replaced that diner with a new one and made a bold statement: He would buy a new diner every five years.

Route 22, Phillipsburg.

The former Avenel Diner on Route 1 in Woodbridge is now (oh, no!) a Subway.

North Wildwood.

By the late forties, Fritz's diner was doing a thousand dollars plus in business daily, terrific numbers for the time. The diner was the darling of Jerry O'Mahony, Inc., its manufacturer. "Styled for Beauty," announced an O'Mahony ad featuring the diner in the July 1947 issue of *The Diner*.

The daily special was written on a billboard that slid into a slot between the two signs atop the diner. The special in the 1947 O'Mahony ad was Hungarian Beef Goulash, with fresh vegetables, rolls, and butter, for fifty cents.

In addition to her regular salary and tips, a waitress at Fritz's earned 10 percent "commission" on her sales over two hundred dollars a week. In the mid-1950s some of the diner's waitresses were making more than five hundred dollars a week. Hustling waitresses, constant promotion, and new ideas added up to a new diner every five years for Fritz.

"Believe it or not," the jug-eared diner man once said, "my diner is so well-organized and staffed it practically operates by itself."

◆ ◆ ◆ 👑 ◆ ◆ ◆

The late forties and early fifties were the golden age of Jersey diners. Each month *The Diner* (later known as *Diner & Counter Restaurant; Diner & Restaurant; Diner Drive-In and Restaurant;* and *Diner Drive-In*) heralded the opening of a dozen or more diners, mostly in New Jersey and New York.

Route 46, Bridgeville. (Courtesy of Ken Parker)

Big Ernie's Diner, Wildwood.

It was a time of peppy waitresses (Agnes of the Rod Diner in Elizabeth sang to customers), crafty owners, and eye-catching signs and buildings. The Tower of Pizza on Route 17 was not the only roadside attraction. Walt's Drive-In on Route 46 in Caldwell had a B-29 tail assembly sticking out of its roof. It had come from a plane that had crashed at nearby Curtiss-Wright Airport.

In *The Diner,* manufacturers didn't need anyone to sing their praises; they did it themselves, in their ads. "Why be content with less when the best is available now?" asked Mountain View. "Good Looking Diners Make More Money," announced Fodero. "First Again with the World's Finest Deluxe Diner," proclaimed Paramount. "America's Smartest Dining Car," boasted Kullman.

Every manufacturer claimed that it had just built "the world's biggest diner." Judging by ads and notices in *The Diner,* a new "world's biggest diner" was going up somewhere every month, if not every week. In one issue, DeRaffele announced "the world's longest, most modern and up-to-date diner," and Kullman "the world's largest diner"— in side-by-side ads.

Being big at anything was worth bragging about. In 1947 Mickey and Fred's Diner on Route 17 in East Rutherford claimed to have the biggest diner parking lot in New Jer-

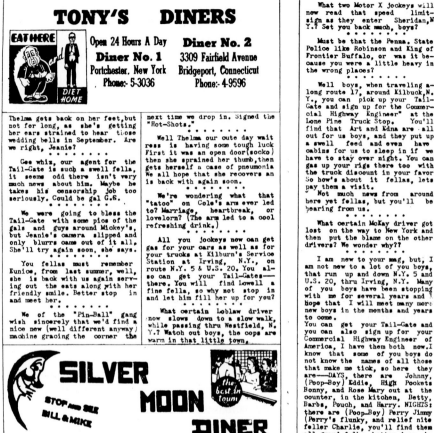

Tail-Gate magazine, July 1950. The monthly magazine provided helpful tips and the latest gossip to truckers up and down the East Coast. (Courtesy of Christine Guedon-DeConcini)

sey. The Suburban Diner in East Orange was not only the world's largest diner, it offered "the world's fastest service."

Diner owners tried many ways to entice patrons—promotions, giveaways, specials, billboards. Few did it better than Leo and Morris Bauman, owners of Newark's famed Weequahic Diner. Customers on the diner's mailing list received birthday and wedding anniversary cards, and miniature holiday menus the week before the events. Every mother received a corsage on Mother's Day.

Children were not forgotten; at the diner they could play with, and take home, colorful cut-out masks. Printed on the back of the masks: the diner's children's specials.

◆ ◆ ◆ 👑 ◆ ◆ ◆

Diners were—and are—a male-dominated world. Women were not even allowed into diners, in fact, until the thirties. "Ladies invited" signs started appearing on diner fronts; some exist to this day, including those at Max's in Harrison and the Summit Diner.

In the forties and fifties, waitresses could be as peppy and personable as they wanted, but they had to know their place, if a column in *Diner & Restaurant* was any indication.

A woman's hair is her crowning glory, but only when it's on her head. When her lovely locks stray all over the place and some of them wind up in the soup or in the salad, the waitress should be crowned with something more formidable than hair.

That wasn't all on the columnist's mind.

Some women think that their beauty increases in direct ratio to the length of their fingernails. If you have one of these babes in your place, speak to her gently but firmly. If her hand ever slips while she's serving a meal, she's likely to inflict twelfth degree lacerations on one of your favorite customers. If you don't do anything about this hazard, don't let her wait on me when I drop in on you. I want a nice peaceful death. I don't want to be clawed to ribbons.

If you ate in a Newark diner in the forties, chances are you ate at Scotty's. "Eat at the Sign of the Scotty Dog," announced matchbooks, referring to the neon-lit dog atop the diner's sign.

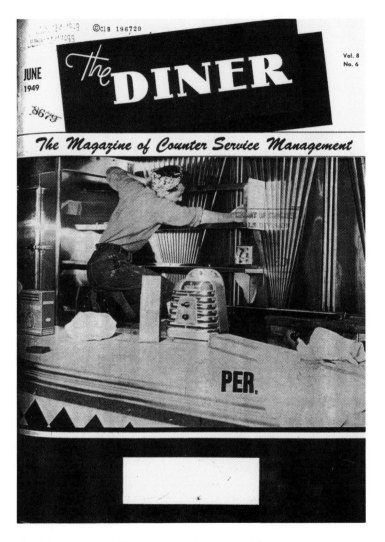

The Diner, *June 1949. The cover shows the old Somerset Diner in Plainfield. The magazine was published under various names from 1940 to 1957.*

The Diner, *August 1949.*

Diner Drive-In & Restaurant, *November 1954.*   Diner Drive-In, *June 1955.*

There were a half dozen Scotty's in and around Newark. The chain was started by Leo Mavraidis and Charley Mesanazos, who had started the Harrison Lunch, and Lou Miles. On Thanksgiving, Christmas, and New Year's, every member of the armed forces got a free meal at Scotty's. Every regular customer received a gift at Christmas.

Bill Marmaras, co-owner of the Harris Diner, worked at two Scotty's—Route 1 in Elizabeth, and 4th Avenue and Mount Pleasant Avenue in Newark—in the 1950s.

"I was the second cook; my cousin was the big chef," he recalls.

"While the owners don't believe in practicing price-cutting, help-snatching and other similar evils of cut-throat dining car operation, they are alert to competition," according to an article in the December 1946 issue of *The Diner*.

"Some time ago, another operator set up a car about half a mile from [Scotty's]. He didn't last long, but rather than have someone who could survive get in there and walk off with some of their business, the boys took over the car and are operating it as a defensive measure."

When Nora Carpenter, a much-publicized English mother of quadruplets, arrived in this country in the mid-forties, she had her first meal on U.S. soil at Scotty's. The first place Mickey Rooney stopped on his return from Europe? At the sign of the Scotty Dog.

◆ ◆ ◆ 👑 ◆ ◆ ◆

"You still puzzling about Accent?" asked the 1949 magazine ad. "It's not a flavoring! It's not a condiment! It's not an ordinary seasoning! It's 99+% PURE MSG . . . a natural product . . . wholesome and good."

No wonder the forties and fifties were a simpler age. We didn't know any better.

It was a time of technological breakthrough, and the diner world was no exception. Time-saving and money-making innovations were heralded in every issue of *The Diner*.

The Hollymatic patty-molding machine ($595) could mold, eject, and stack eighteen hundred patties an hour on waxed paper. The Chef-Master Deluxe Hot Dogger ($73.50) could steam two hundred franks "to tender plumpness" and fifty buns to "bakery freshness."

The Lindavap Corp. of Ann Arbor, Michigan, offered an "insect eradicator" called the New Bug-Git, while the Carand Corp. of Racine, Wisconsin, made an airborne germ vaporizer called the Microbomb. Dow Chemical even sold a calcium chloride mix to cut down dust at drive-ins.

In keeping with the times, products emphasized speed and efficiency. Savory toast-makers produced up to twelve slices of toast per minute, at an operating cost of "a few pennies per hour." Armour Steakettes came frozen but could be fried or grilled in ninety seconds. Ads for Procter & Gamble's deep-fryer, the Fryarama, emphasized that it was fast and economical.

Asbury Park–based Tradio offered the Tradio-ette, "the smallest coin-operated radio in the world," a wall-mounted unit with built-in antenna and a preset volume control so you couldn't disturb someone in the next booth. For ten cents, you'd get fifteen minutes' worth of radio.

Some ads looked as if they came straight from today's *National Enquirer.* "Delicious Mashed Potatoes in 2 Minutes!" began an ad for French's Instant Potato. "'A Miracle!' says Lawrence Cooper, proprietor of Cooper's Restaurants, Memphis, Tenn."

Grease wasn't the word, eye appeal was. Looking for a guaranteed crowd pleaser? Try the Pig's Dinner, an ice-cream dish served in a disposable paper trough decorated with dancing pigs. A Portland, Oregon, firm advertised Pronto Pups, hot dogs dipped into Pronto Pup batter and then deep-fried for three minutes.

A pound of Whitato, an antioxidant, kept up to 3,200 pounds of potatoes white. Glorified Steak Mold shaped ordinary ground beef to resemble T-bone or sirloin.

Food companies had plenty of recipes and hints for diner owners and home cooks. Kraft offered its "Cheez Whiz Rabbit Specialty." Heat Cheez Whiz on a steam table or double boiler, place broiled tomato halves on toast squares, pour hot Cheez Whiz over each tomato half, and top with broiled bacon strips. One Cheez Whiz Rabbit coming up.

It was the age of electronics and the dawn of the space age, and the products reflected the American fascination with both. In 1951, for example, Downyflake offered a "revolutionary new" Waffle Robot, while Providence-based Money-Meters Inc. advertised a RobotCashier.

The Star Manufacturing Co. in St. Louis carried the space-age theme to near-delirious heights. Ads for the company's Star-Master line of griddles and fryers featured a comely Space Girl with a see-through helmet, a star-bedecked short skirt cinched with

Not a bad slogan for diners everywhere. Garfield.

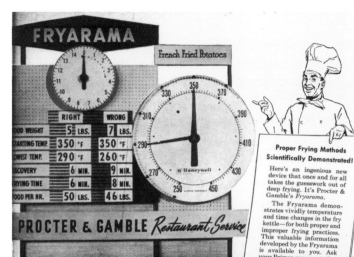

FRYARAMA

French Fried Potatoes

	RIGHT	WRONG
FOOD WEIGHT	5½ LBS.	7 LBS.
STARTING TEMP.	350 °F	350 °F
LOWEST TEMP.	290 °F	260 °F
RECOVERY	6 MIN.	9 MIN.
FRYING TIME	6 MIN.	8 MIN.
FOOD PER HR.	50 LBS.	46 LBS.

PROCTER & GAMBLE *Restaurant Service*

Proper Frying Methods Scientifically Demonstrated!

Here's an ingenious new device that once and for all takes the guesswork out of deep frying. It's Procter & Gamble's *Fryarama*.

The Fryarama demonstrates vividly temperature and time changes in the fry kettle—for both proper and improper frying practices. This valuable information developed by the Fryarama is available to you. Ask your Primex representative for full details.

The Fryarama showed the "Whys" of Good Deep Frying!

Deep frying is a live subject with restaurant operators these days for three good reasons: 1) It's fast. 2) It's economical. (There's minimum waste since food is prepared only on order.) 3) Properly fried foods are proved patron pleasers.

In this connection you will be interested to know that the research staff of the Procter & Gamble Restaurant Kitchens has developed a scientific device—the Fryarama—which shows exactly what goes on in the fry kettle.

The Fryarama was demonstrated at the recent NRA Show in Chicago. Viewers of the demonstration saw, for example, visible proof of the *dangers and false economy of overloading the fry kettles*. The Fryarama proved that this practice slows up frying time, slows down production and tends to increase fat absorption. Definite evidence of the need for using proper frying methods!

But, as important as correct frying procedures are, *you've also got to use a good frying fat to produce good fried foods*. That's why so many successful eating places use pure, bland, all-vegetable Primex for all their frying.

ALL-VEGETABLE
ALL-HYDROGENATED

PRIMEX

The "Longer Frying Life" Fat

★ MADE BY PROCTER & GAMBLE — USED BY THOUSANDS OF SUCCESSFUL RESTAURANTS ★

. . . for more details circle 145 on last page

Fryarama ad, Diner Drive-In, *September 1955.*

star puts the heat where it counts

starmaster griddles

Both Gas and Electric Models Available

...ting news from Starmaster! It's the ultramodern Star-...ster Heat Trap Griddle that really puts the heat on old-...ioned cooking methods. Only Starmaster griddles act-...y trap the heat and keep it right on the griddle, where ...ounts. Starmaster griddles cook faster, cheaper, and ...r than any other griddle on the market. Has exception-

...ally low pre-heat time. Heavy-duty steel plate griddles can't crack or warp. In smart design, top performance, and low, low price, it's Starmaster for 1957. But don't take our word for it . . . better go see the biggest equipment value of any year. That's Starmaster Heat Trap Griddles. There's a Starmaster Matched Line unit for every counter cooking need.

★ STAR

...R MANUFACTURING COMPANY • ST. LOUIS 20, MO. • Division of Hercules Galion Products, Inc.
Canadian Distributor: CROWN ELECTRICAL MFG., LTD. • BRANTFORD, ONTARIO, CANADA

- - - for more details circle 149 on last page

Diner Drive-In, *February 1957.*

Colonial Diner, Lyndhurst.

a star-embroidered belt, and high white boots stitched with you-know-what along the sides.

"Out-of-this-world values," the ad proclaimed.

A 1955 issue of *Diner Drive-In* contained news of an out-of-this-world meal. In a demonstration, food industry representatives cooked breakfast at the site of an atomic bomb test outside Las Vegas. The next day—4,500 feet from Ground Zero—they served a lunch of Irish beef stew, beef sandwiches, baked beans, apples, ice cream, coffee, and milk.

"This will be the first time," the magazine noted, "that a meal will be served under atomic blast conditions."

HERE ARE SOME HELPFUL HINTS FROM THE PAGES OF *THE DINER* IN THE LATE FORTIES AND EARLY FIFTIES:

Does your hambone-flavored pea soup remind your customers of the salt sea breezes of their hitch in the Navy? Cook a potato along with the bone and your soup will cure this. (*The Diner*, FEBRUARY 1949)

Vary the shape of your meat patties. Oblong, square or wedged-shaped patties lend interest to the platter after a routine of the usual round one. (*The Diner*, OCTOBER 1949)

If your soups and gravies aren't going over the way you think they ought to, maybe you should make the acquaintance of MSG (monosodium glutamate). (*The Diner*, NOVEMBER 1949)

Some corny rhymester has told us that:
"Apple pie without the cheese
is like a kiss without the squeeze."
An inexpensive way of adding the cheese flavor to apple pie is to roll grated cheese in the crust before baking. (*The Diner*, APRIL 1949)

Hamburgers and frankfurters that are cooked on a griddle develop a real come-again flavor if a small, heavy-oak board is placed on them while they are sizzling. (*The Diner*, JUNE 1949)

Fancy tongue dish for display and service comes when you steam it or cook it in water until almost done, then stick it with whole cloves, spread with prepared mustard and cover with brown sugar. Bake in moderate oven, 350 degrees, one hour. Call it Glazed Tongue on the menu. (*Diner & Counter Restaurant*, DECEMBER 1951)

If any liquid is spilled, don't wait to wipe it up because you're busy. And go easy on the floor wax. Lots of shine may mean a hurt behin'! (*The Diner*, MARCH 1950)

If you're thinking about redecorating, remember the psychological effects of color. Yellow is cheerful, pinks and blues are restful, as is green. White conveys an undesirable hospital impression. (*The Diner*, APRIL 1950)

We're not plugging soap or frightening you by booming "B.O.," but it is important in summer time to be particularly careful not to offend. Uniforms must be changed oftener to avoid unpleasant body odor from perspiration. (*The Diner*, JUNE 1947)

The most appetizing color for restaurant walls under all types of lighting, psychologists tell us, is peach. Other appetite-stimulating colors are turquoise blue, light coral and bright yellow. (*The Diner*, SEPTEMBER 1949)

A thin layer of cream or milk over the top of white sauce will keep scum from forming. (*The Diner*, DECEMBER 1947)

The alert operator will look to his garbage to lower his food costs. You'd be surprised what you'll find in addition to your normal waste. (*The Diner*, JANUARY 1947)

Stale bread can be freshened by covering it with a damp cloth and putting it into the oven for about ten minutes. (*Diner & Restaurant*, MARCH 1953)

Warm weather wears nerves ragged. Therefore, be especially courteous to your customers during the summer months. You've got to humor those elusive summer dollars. (*The Diner*, AUGUST 1946)

What's in your window? A few tired streamers of crepe paper and a fake sundae? The best come-on to doubtful customers is heaps of attractive baked goods or other foods that make customers want to come in. (*Diner & Counter Restaurant*, OCTOBER 1951)

It takes rinse water at a temperature of 180 degrees or higher to have any effect on germs. (*The Diner*, FEBRUARY 1947)

You're not being economical when you buy those midget-sized napkins. Since most men don't take a delicate dab at their lips with a napkin, it's probable they'll use three or four napkins before the meal is over. (*The Diner*, JULY 1947)

Individuals who are very tall, very short, very thin or very fat do not make as good restaurant employees as people of average height and normal weight. (*Diner & Restaurant*, AUGUST 1952)

Fresh fish: Shiny eyes, firm flesh, gills bright and red, fresh odor, sinks in water. (*The Diner*, MARCH 1948)

Coffee has probably affected restaurant profits more than any other single factor. Good coffee keeps old customers and makes new ones; poor coffee drives the customer away. (*The Diner*, NOVEMBER 1947)

MANNA-OR MANA-FROM HEAVEN

Ala Haddadin, cook, White Mana, Jersey City.

One's in Hackensack, the other's in Jersey City.

One's across the street from a McDonald's, the other's down the road from Hub-cap Heaven.

One's located next to a lake, the other's located on a busy stretch of one of the state's busiest roads.

One came direct from the 1939 New York World's Fair, the other came direct from the 1939 New York World's Fair.

Wait a minute. How could they *both* come from the World's Fair?

"You know this came from the World's Fair," says White Manna co-owner Ronnie Cohen, pointing to a newspaper story saying so.

"The one in Hackensack," says White Mana owner Mario Costa, "has nothing to do with the World's Fair."

The evidence supports Costa, although newspaper stories keep referring to the Hackensack White Manna as the World's Fair relic.

"The original White Manna . . . was exhibited at the 1939 World's Fair in New York," according to Jeffrey Tennyson, author of *Hamburger Heaven* (Hyperion, 1993). "It was later moved to Jersey City."

The Hackensack White Manna is smaller and much more photogenic; the beautiful little red-and-white diner has appeared on the covers of several books, including my own *Roadside New Jersey* (Rutgers University Press, 1994).

The White Mana's fluorescent-lit, oval-shaped interior was visited by thousands of people at the 1939 New York World's Fair.

The White Mana, on the other hand, is a stylistic mishmash: the original white porcelain orange-trimmed front is now bricked over and the dining room expanded, although the HAMBURGERS SINCE 1946 and CURB SERVICE signs remain.

A 1995 *New York Times* story profiled five Jersey diners. Guess which one of the Mannas the paper picked?

"The reporter probably never even heard of us," Mario grumbles.

But many people have, because somebody is buying the three thousand burgers the White Mana sells every week (the White Manna sells about three thousand a week, too, according to Cohen).

And the White Mana had one thing the White Manna never had: curbside service. Several of the girls who worked the parking lot were burlesque performers at the Hudson Theater in Union City.

Larry McMillen, cook, White Mana, Jersey City.

House rules, White Mana, Jersey City.

Many people would be surprised to discover that the White Mana and White Manna were started by the same man.

He was Louis Bridges, who opened five White Mannas in the mid-forties—in Jersey City, Hackensack, Elizabeth, and Springfield.

The White Mana, a Kullman, opened for business on June 2, 1946, on Tonnele Avenue (Route 1) in Jersey City. Louis Bridges started the minichain, but his brother, Webster, would soon take over the operation.

"This was the introduction to fast food at the World's Fair," says Mario, relaying what Web Bridges told him. "The whole idea was three steps. The person behind the

White Mana, Jersey City.

counter does not have to take more than three steps to cook the food and get your soft drink."

"In the forties you had the White Mana, the White Orchard on Kennedy Boulevard, a White Castle in North Bergen, and a small Astro Burger on Sip Avenue and 440," recalls White Mana regular William Clark.

"In the forties, all the diners around here were 'White'—White Diamond, White Circle," Mario explains. "Then it changed to 'Orange' [Orange Circle, for example]. Web told me orange was a color that made people eat." He laughs. "Or relaxed them, I don't know."

"Hamburgers here were never lower than a dime," Clark says. "It was a dime, two for fifteen cents, then two for a quarter. You used to get the largest bag of french fries for ten cents. In this big wax bag."

Mario, who grew up in Newark, heard about the White Mana through one of his bosses at the Holiday Inn at Newark Airport, where he worked; the man's brother was married to Bridges's daughter. Until that time Mario thought the White Mana was a "big place where they had weddings."

When Mario first came here, the diner was called the White Manna, like the others. Somehow, it lost an *n* over the years. Even Mario is not sure why.

"Why they drop one, I don't know," he says, "Maybe easier to spell. They both mean the same thing—bread from heaven."

He started working at the diner in 1972 as a cleanup man, making $1.67 an hour. By the time he graduated from college, he had saved more than thirty thousand dollars.

In 1979 Bridges wanted out; he was convinced fast-food restaurants were the future. He sold the White Mana to Mario for eighty thousand dollars and opened a fast-food place—the White Manor—right across the street. It didn't last long.

Mario was twenty-three when he became the White Mana's owner.

"I used to tell everyone I was twenty-nine, so I could get a little respect," says the diner owner, who bears a resemblance to actor Al Pacino. "I used to wear a mustache to make me look older. But I was a baby."

His college buddies would stop at the Mana on their way back from the shore, see Mario in his white pants, white shirt, and white cap, and laugh. They're not laughing now. Mario also owns Ringside, a sports bar across the highway.

Among those who have stopped here over the years: Chuck Berry and Mike Tyson.

In the fifties, according to former waitress Joan Turino, the White Mana was a "hopping" place, offering curb service until five A.M. The waitresses could make one hundred dollars on a Friday or Saturday night back then.

Dig that crazy floor! The White Mana's tiled floor is one of the most distinctive anywhere.

Mario says actor Dustin Hoffman drove up in a car once and sent someone in for a couple of burgers.

The White Mana has changed over the years, but the horsehoe-shaped counter remains, and so does one tradition.

"Coffee's still free for the cops," Mario says. "They have to pay for the cake, though."

One other devoted White Mana follower deserves mention. He was Tony DiGiglio, brother of reputed Jersey organized crime boss John DiGiglio.

Even after he developed cancer and was confined to his home, DiGiglio would send his daughter down to White Mana for some burgers.

At DiGiglio's funeral, his wife told Mario that her husband couldn't eat anything in his final days but still asked for a couple of White Mana burgers.

He couldn't eat them, but at least he wanted to smell them.

♦ ♦ ♦ ♛ ♦ ♦ ♦

"How we got here?" asks Ronnie Cohen, standing, spatula in hand, behind the tiny grill in the White Manna.

"My brother used to have an Israeli restaurant in Fair Lawn. I worked for a kosher deli. This place was on the market. We went for it. I think we are happy."

He and his brother, Ofer, bought the White Manna from longtime owner John Aldridge in 1985.

"Better service, better attitude," one regular says of the change in ownership. "The guy who used to own it, John, had a bad attitude."

"He was here forty years," Ronnie says diplomatically. "I don't know how I would react after forty years."

You can't help but smile as you walk into the White Manna. It is so small you'd think it was built to kid scale. Twenty stools are distributed around the U-shaped counter and two window nooks. The grill is right in front of you.

Outside, the red-trimmed glass block, the stainless-steel door, the white roof and panels, and red WHITE MANNA sign make for the postcard-prettiest diner in the state.

"It's remarkable how much money that little thing has made," jokes regular Don

Co-owner Ronnie Cohen makes a hamburger for an eager customer inside the tiny White Manna, the "Fenway Park" of diners, according to Will Anderson, author of Mid-Atlantic Roadside Delights.

Marcone, pointing to the grill. "Millions of dollars, that little goddamn thing. Re-markable."

Ronnie hasn't made millions; otherwise he wouldn't be working here from 7 A.M. to 6 P.M. Mondays through Fridays and 7 A.M. to 4 P.M. Saturdays.

"I was in Laguna Beach [California]," Stan Kotkin of Teaneck recalls. "I was in this gallery. They had a print of this place. I was thumbing through the prints, saw it, couldn't believe it. The girl at the gallery said it was one of their best-selling prints."

"Businesswise, it's a simple business to run," Ronnie says. "No overhead."

"Then after six months," smiles Marcone, "he made his first million. This is what people tell me on the street."

Those on the street say the White Manna has good burgers. They're nice and juicy, and cooked right in front of you. In fact, both the Mana and Manna are known for their burgers. "A White Manna lunatic," says Marcone, looking across the street at the McDonald's, "will not go over there even when this place is crowded. He'd rather starve."

In *The Primal Cheeseburger* (Viking Penguin, 1994), Elisabeth Rozin imagines when primitive people first realized that the browning of meat and the liquefaction of fat made for an unbeatable combination. It is prehistoric times. A small band of hunters trudges across the savannah, skirting a grass fire. Suddenly their leader, an elderly female, sniffs the air. They follow the smell to its source—a crippled gazelle, slowly roasting on burning stubble. The leader pokes at the carcass with a stick. The aroma is wonderful. She hacks off a chunk of meat, sniffs it, takes a lick, and then a bite. The skin is browned and crispy, and the warm meat is running with juice and fat, far more tender than anything she has ever tasted.

And that, Rozin speculates, is how our beloved greasy burger may have gotten its start.

Those who swear by the Manna's—or the Mana's—burgers don't care if the first burger came from a gazelle, a brontosaurus, or a prehistoric chain of fast-food joints; all that matters is that they taste good.

After flipping his last burger of the day, Ronnie closes the place. He is enjoying a cigarette when a friend walks in, jubilant.

"Ronnie," the man says with a thick Polish accent, "I am father today."

"Mazel tov," Ronnie says. "Boy or girl?"

"Boy," says his friend, still wearing a hospital bracelet. "Nine pounds, four ounces."

"Hungry baby," Ronnie observes.

Miss America Diner, Jersey City

DREAMING OF DINERS

*T*wenty years later John Baeder still remembers that dream.

Stirred by childhood memories of what he saw from the train that took him every summer from his parents' home in Atlanta to South Bend, Indiana, he started chronicling, in the seventies, the American roadside.

Initially he did paintings of the postcards of gas stations, tourist courts, motels, and other roadside Americana he had collected. Then he started photographing the one feature of the American landscape that intrigued him most—diners.

One night he had a dream about a diner painted in a color he calls "landlord green." Several months later he took one of his frequent drives from New York City, where he then lived, into New Jersey.

"I'd just drive, get lost sometimes," he recalls, sitting in an outdoor café in Lambertville. "I'm driving down this road, getting tired, time for a break, and suddenly there's this Silk City diner in landlord green in front of me.

"It was my dream come true. I never did a painting of it, but it always haunted me."

If Baeder was looking for a sign that he was on the right artistic track, he certainly got it. In 1978 his book *Diners* (Harry N. Abrams), a collection of diner paintings, was published. It was a seminal work in the field; Richard Gutman and Elliott Kaufman's landmark book, *American Diner* (Harper & Row, 1979), often credited for sparking a nationwide interest in diners, would follow a year later.

If Gutman is the Einstein of diners—he seems to know something about every

John Baeder, Rosie's Diner, *oil on canvas, 1979.* (Courtesy of the artist)

diner ever made—Baeder is their Matisse, capturing their allure in images. Both authors have published sequels to their books; Gutman's *American Diner Then and Now* (HarperCollins) in 1993, Baeder's *Diners* (Harry N. Abrams) in 1995.

"I am moved by diners," Baeder writes in the more recent book. "It cannot be explained. Diners 'talk' to me for a number of reasons."

On his first visit to Chappy's, he was impressed with the Paterson diner's "rhythm."

"Subtly," he wrote, "it reminded me of a collage."

While his writing may not be for everyone—in one paragraph he talks about Father Sky and Mother Earth, and in the next paragraph he quotes Aeschylus—he never forgets what diners, at their most basic, are about:

John Baeder, Pappy's, Union Boulevard, Wayne, *watercolor on paper, 1990. Formerly the White Way and the Boulevard, now a restaurant.* (Courtesy of the artist)

John Baeder, Blue Beacon, Newark, *oil on canvas, 1980. "Its blue light sent signals of comfort to locals and passersby," he writes.* (Courtesy of the artist)

I tend to judge a diner's food quality by first checking out how clean the grill is, then the home fries that are prepared on that grill—my criteria, maybe not yours. I don't care. The Bendix Diner on Route 17 . . . has home fries that become instant friends with your taste buds.

"New Jersey has always been the richest experience for me," the artist says, swatting away gnats in the outdoor café. "Jersey is a vast arena of visual delights."
Of the ninety-five diners in the revised *Diners,* twenty are from New Jersey, in-

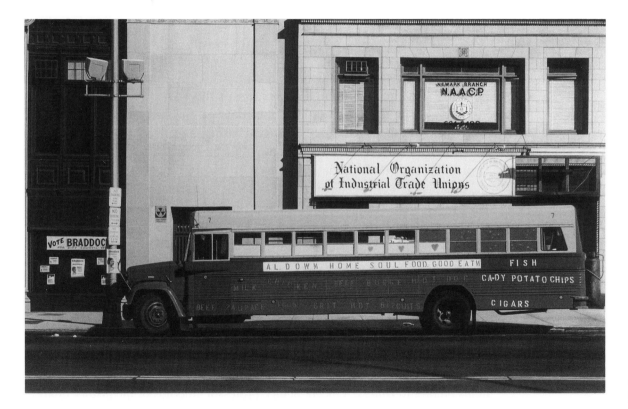

John Baeder, Newark.
(Courtesy of the artist)

cluding Max's in Harrison, John's Diner (now the Hammonton Diner) in Hammonton, the Tick-Tock Diner in Clifton, and the long-gone Blue Beacon in Newark.

Baeder's first painting of any kind was of a White Tower in Camden. His "pivotal" diner painting, the former Highway Diner in Burlington, was done in 1973.

He had just met Gutman; the two, plus Kaufman and architect David Slovik, were a kind of diner circle back then, exchanging ideas, showing their slides and memorabilia.

"The sparks," Baeder recalls, "were flying."

At their first meeting Gutman showed him a photo of the Highway Diner. Baeder painted it in black and white, the diner sleek and streamlined, cars—the year is about 1945—parked out front.

"It was at that point," Baeder says, "that I began to pursue the diner as subject matter."

He remembered, as a five-year-old boy living with his sister, parents, and grandparents in the Biltmore Hotel in Atlanta, how wonderful a diner could be.

He would walk into the Majestic Diner, across the street from the hotel, and sit at the counter, where he always felt bigger than normal because the counter was low. He'd watch the short-order cook perform: "He'd throw the red blob of meat on the grill. Sizzle. Down went the spatula. Flip; there went the buns on the searing grill. Another spatula press. A louder sizzzzzzle. Up came the fries, twist went the basket, swoosh went the plate. A twist of the body and they were on the counter. Clunk."

The curly-haired artist, dressed in his familiar blue jeans and blue denim shirt, pauses for a moment in the café. He acknowledges that what he is about to say is "deep," but he's going to say it anyway. Jung's theory was that everyone had a masculine and feminine side. For Baeder, diners represent his feminine side.

"The door is the vagina, the grill the hearth. Jung would call it the Great Mother." He laughs. "It sounds like a lot of pretentious bullshit. But my work has more soul and depth because of that. That's the bottom stuff, the deep-bottom stuff."

In *Diners,* he puts it another way: "I find sacredness in diners. An important religious rite in early religions was the marriage of Earth and Sky. The diner is the Mother symbol—the great provider."

In his preface to *Diners,* Vincent Scully, professor emeritus of the history of art at Yale University, says that Baeder's paintings differ from those of most of his photo-realist or magic-realist contemporaries.

John Baeder, Old Diner, Musi Plant. (Courtesy of the artist)

"Baeder is not haunted like Hopper by a sense of something empty, hollow and solitary in the American experience. Instead, he is youthful, hopeful, a painter-poet who makes us see the beauty of common things. . . ."

Not everyone likes Baeder's realist paintings. But his work seems much closer to the spirit of diners than do most photographs on the subject.

He flips through my photos on the café table, looking for new diner images, for new inspiration. His eyes widen when he sees the Orange Circle in Orange; he's never seen it before, and loves it. "How long would it take to get there?" he immediately wants to know.

His most recent book, *Sign Language,* is a collection of two hundred photos of homemade signs around the country. It is the distillation of thirty years' work. But diners will always be special to him; they speak in mysterious and wonderful ways.

"There were only six stools at the counter, four at the window side," he recalls of a visit to the Short Stop, then in Belleville. "I look around this cutesy little place and realize why it's named the Short Stop. I watch Hazel take teensy ground beef balls from a teensy storage space behind a teensy aluminum door, plop, mash, sizzle on a teensy grill. Serve the teensy burgers on teensy paper plates. No fuss. The short stop and short order."

WHITE CIRCLE SYSTEM, 5 P.M.

Vinnie Ciccone, longtime White Circle System customer. "I remember when they served coffee in jars," he recalls.

Paul Celeste—cook, manager, chief bottle washer, and potato slicer in the pleasantly seedy White Circle System in Bloomfield—acts as if this is the last place on earth he wants to be.

But underneath the tough-guy veneer—pack of cigarettes in a rolled-up sleeve, permanent scowl on his face—is a man committed to his work, even if he seems to consider it a notch above sewer cleaner among the least-glamorous jobs.

"I've been here since August 16, 1980," he says by way of introduction. "It was a Wednesday, I think."

It doesn't take much to get him talking.

"Blue Castle, I worked before this. We had six of those. Worked at every one. Kearny, Union, Newark—two in Newark—Jersey City, and Passaic."

He pauses. "You want to take pictures of the joint?"

"Like to."

"You can do anything you want. You can wait on the customers if you want."

"I've been coming here thirty years," pipes up a droopy-eyed Vinnie Ciccone, wearing a sweater and rakish cap. "I remember when they served coffee in jars."

"You got two cups for the price of one," Paul says. "It stayed hot for hours. Cost a quarter—nickel deposit."

"There were a lot of factories around here," says Vinnie, looking up Bloomfield Avenue. "Lysol, General Motors, Westinghouse. You had a paper box company, too."

You can't beat the prices: two eggs, toast, coffee, and home fries for under two bucks at the White Circle System, Bloomfield Avenue, Bloomfield.

"Ninety-nine percent of the guys who work here are drunks," Paul announces. "I worked with four hundred guys, 99 percent of them drunks. Most of us are alcoholics, or real heavy drinkers. To tell you the truth, you ever see a short-order cook who didn't drink, you're looking at God."

"You're not an alcoholic," Vinnie says.

"I'm getting there," Paul says.

How did he end up in a place like this?

A smile briefly replaces the scowl. "As your career goes down, down, down. . . . I worked in a deli, cafeteria, three hamburger joints. I almost got murdered behind the counter three times. I got all cut up here"—he points to his arm—"couldn't move it for a month. Gun to the head twice. Other than that it's been lovely."

"Lot of drifters come in here now," Vinnie says. "It's a good place to stop. They don't bother nobody. You meet all kinds of characters here. You meet the real people."

The diner—beautiful and shiny on the outside, with a downward-pointing arrow that wraps around the words "White Circle"—was built in 1954 by the Manno Dining Car Co., then in Belleville. There were three other White Circles—here and in Newark and Springfield. There is an identical-looking Orange Circle in Orange. But the White Circle, unlike the Orange Circle, is open twenty-four hours every day.

"The first twenty-four hours," Paul cracks, "are the hardest."

Paul Celeste, cook and manager at the White Circle System. "You ever see a short-order cook who didn't drink," he says, "you're looking at God."

Diner still life, White Circle System: waffle irons, can of Pam, fire extinguisher, juice squeezer.

"This is the only place in New Jersey," insists Vinnie, "where you can get fresh-squeezed orange juice. They squeeze it right in front of you."

Paul, cigarette dangling precariously to one side, reaches under the grill and removes the grease tray, filled with all sorts of unidentifiable charred stuff.

Two cast-iron waffle makers are on the back counter, right next to the fire extinguisher and the juice squeezer.

"I eat breakfast here every day, the special," Vinnie says. Two eggs, potatoes, toast, and coffee: under two bucks.

"Reasonable prices," I observe.

"They just raised them," Vinnie grumbles. "They were cheaper."

Paul takes out a spatula and starts chopping onions.

"Everything is homemade here," Vinnie says.

"Including the help," Paul adds. "Vinnie, do me a favor. Go out to my car and unlock the trunk."

"And get the gun out?" Vinnie asks, smiling.

At this point one is not sure who's the comedian and who's the straight man.

Vinnie comes back with a roll of black electrical tape, which Paul uses to tape up his spatula. Vinnie starts sweeping the floor.

"I've got to sleep here tonight," he explains. "I'm trying to make it nice."

Paul says his uncle is somebody called Richie the Boot.

"I never bothered with those people," he says. "I didn't want to get killed."

A cryptic note above the register reads: Apple pie ———.

"You know what's wrong with our money?" Paul asks. "It's all the same color. Wrong. You go to other countries, it's all different-colored bills. And you have different pictures on each one. Pictures of banks, saloons, whatever.

Paul Celeste peels potatoes at the White Circle System. The diner goes through 150 pounds of burgers and sixty dozen eggs a week.

The White Circle System may have seen better days, but how many other places offer fresh-squeezed orange juice?

"What they need in this country is a nice Italian president," he adds. "Straighten this mess up in a hurry."

"Where the hell they going to find this person?" asks Bill, another regular. "Remember the guy Diogenes?"

Is this a greasy spoon, you wonder, or humanities class?

"What do you like most about this job?"

"When I work by myself," Paul replies. "The least? Trying to keep up with it. With the boss, the help, all this"—he looks up and down the counter—"crap. It doesn't look like much but believe me it ain't no friggin' picnic."

The diner goes through 150 pounds of burgers and sixty dozen eggs a week.

Vinnie, sixty-six, retired from Hoffman-LaRoche, caddies now and then to stay fit.

"I watch what I eat," he says. "I don't smoke. I had a beer the other day in Montclair."

Paul goes off to slice up some potatoes.

"Here comes the Wolfman," Vinnie announces.

"Charlie Manson's brother," Paul says.

In walks a big guy with a thick black beard and socks up to his knees. The look is not so much Charlie Manson as Rasputin. He opens a box of brand-new sneakers. Size 10 1/2. Anyone want to buy them?

Wolfman leaves. Paul tells a story.

"Guy walked in one day, summer day. Walks in with a big overcoat. Okay. Stands there, takes out a piece of paper, plain white piece of paper. Writes down these hieroglyphics, not like Scrabble, but neat. Hands me the piece of paper and walks out. Didn't say a word. Never saw him again."

One more question. "People come here for the food or because it's a good place to hang out?"

"If they came for the food," says Paul, lighting another cigarette, "they'd be foolish."

Orange Circle, Orange.

Bart LoBrace attacks a burger at the White Diamond, Elizabeth.

Dewey Conrad, Sunday-morning regular,
White Diamond, Elizabeth.

The venerable Pop 'n' Joe's on Main Avenue in
Clifton became, in mid-1995 . . .

. . . the Sizzle Grill Diner.

West Twenty-first Street, Linden.

Susan Hess of Ocean City enjoys a pickle at the Time Out Diner, Tuckahoe.

Diner or office building? Shore Diner, Tilton Road, Pleasantville.

YOUNG AT HEART

here do they get their energy, these diner old-timers who slave over hot stoves while sensible people their age are out on the golf course or riding air-conditioned buses to Atlantic City?

"I want to retire years ago," says Frank Seretis, the sixty-eight-year-old owner of Tom's Diner on the Ledgewood Circle. "I stay away three, four years, I go crazy. I come back, I feel better."

"I feel like I should be here," says Angie Perry, the seventy-seven-year-old owner of Angie's Bridgeton Grill.

"I'm sixty-seven. What the hell, how much longer you gonna work?" asks Tony Iliadis, owner of Tony's Freehold Grille. "But right now, I feel good. I don't see no reason to quit."

If he quit, there might be mass picketing in downtown Freehold.

"As far as throwing people out, I don't care who you are," he says with a bluster. "If you're not behaving, I'll throw you out."

There's tough-guy Tony, and there's lovable Tony, the one the regulars usually get. He came to the United States in 1947, worked for his uncle at the Matawan Diner, got a job at a rug mill.

"Hamburger and coffee and french fries, for God's sake, was a quarter back in 1955," he says in a voice that can be heard easily above the morning din. "Coca-Cola was a nickel, hamburger was ten cents, and french fries was ten cents. And I'm talking about a quarter-pounder, for God's sake."

Freehold Grille owner Tony Iliadis and his wife.

Above: Tom's Diner, on the Ledgewood Circle (Route 46), where the video for Cyndi Lauper's Time After Time *was filmed.*

Left: The Freehold Grille. "In all my years here," says owner Tony Iliadis, "I cooked twenty-six million eggs."

Tom's Diner, Route 46, Ledgewood Circle.

In the early fifties, he worked as a counterman at the Freehold Grille.

"I don't know how to say it," he says. "Working here was like a natural thing."

Around 1960 George and Angelo Floratos and Mike DeCesare bought the diner. In 1963 Tony became a partner with Mike, buying out George and Angelo. In 1970, he bought out Mike.

"I stand right across the street and watched them put it here," he says of the diner's first day in Freehold. "I looked at this diner and said, man, I would love to own it."

In 1986, he signed the diner over to his three sons, Tom, Pete, and Elias, but Tony is still very much in charge.

"[Until] 1989 I was working from four in the morning to twelve midnight," he says. "When you've got three kids to put through college, you've really got to hustle."

He's slacked off since then. His work day now runs from four to eleven A.M.—seven days a week.

"I had people come every day here from Camden for two years," he says. "They musta died." He laughs. "I didn't kill them."

The other day he did something he had wanted to do for a long time, and the results astonished him.

"I figured it out," he says, a big smile on his face. "In all my years here, I cooked twenty-six million eggs."

Somewhere at the other end of the emotional spectrum is the owner of Tom's Diner. You'd expect a guy whose diner was selected for a hot music video to be a slick, "happening" guy.

But Frank hadn't even heard of the rock star in question when a producer asked permission to use the diner. So he said no.

"My son said, 'Dad, what's her name?' 'Cyndi Lauper.' 'Dad, she's famous, give it to her.'"

That's how Tom's Diner became the setting for the video *Time After Time.*

Frank bought the Silk City diner in 1958 with his father, Tom. In the forties the diner was known as the Silver Dollar. This is where the story gets confusing, so pay attention. The name, but not the diner, moved across the highway, to a new diner. The old Silver Dollar became the Silver Moon. When Frank, a former dishwasher at Paul's Diner in Mountain Lakes, bought the Silver Moon in 1958, he renamed it Tom's, after his son and dad. The Silver Dollar burned down in the late fifties.

"Lots cost three hundred dollars back then, homes, fourteen thousand," Frank says. "You should see the homes back there now. Five-hundred-thousand dollar homes."

He's the short-order cook, while his wife, Pauline ("she married the job"), is the chef.

"She makes the best rice pudding around," he says.

The waitresses include the fiery Maria Rastiello ("When I come to work at five A.M., I sing and dance") and Blondie (Maryanne Hine), who is not to be confused with Young Blondie (Barbara Murgolo).

The specials are attached to the wall with electrical tape. Turkey burgers: $1.85. "New at Tom's," reads a grease-stained message. "Mozzarella sticks, only $1.75."

A man walks in, obviously lost.

"I see a sign that says East 10 but I want to go West 10," he says. "What did I do wrong?"

Frank puts his hand on the man's shoulder, gives him directions.

Forty years and thousands of hours show on Frank's face, and it sounds like he's had enough.

"It's a tough business, very tough," he says. "A lot of people are not working, no money. I get letters from plumbers, carpenters down in South Jersey—'Are there any jobs up here?' Even people who live around here, they come in: 'Frank, there's no work.'

"When you publish that book . . ." he says, hesitating.

"I'll send you a copy."

"If I'm around," he says resignedly.

◆ ◆ ◆ 👑 ◆ ◆ ◆

Down at the Bridgeton Grill, Angie Perry—frail-looking, slightly stooped, gray hair piled atop her head—puts down the broom she has been using to sweep the floor.

She used to work all day, she tells me; now she comes in at 3:00 A.M. and works until 10:30, 11:00 A.M.

Keoki Keanu-Snyder sweeps the floor at the end of another day at the Time Out Diner in Tuckahoe.

"I put in my seven, eight hours," she says quickly, as if her stamina is being questioned.

The diner opened on June 1, 1940. In 1948 Angie, then twenty-nine, bought the Cohansey Grill on Pearl Street. It moved farther up the street, then burned down in the mid-fifties. In 1957 Angie sold her share in the luncheonette to her brother and bought the Bridgeton Grill.

"I was just interested in a diner," she says. "I just wanted to get out on my own."

There were several diners in Bridgeton at the time—the Jersey Diner, Fisher's Diner, the Lyric, the Barbecue, and the Marquette Diner.

"Everybody was really busy then," she recalls. "There were more people living in town. There was more industry. During tomato season it was really busy. Used to have trucks lined up along on Broad Street waiting to get in the packing houses. In the meantime, they came in to eat."

Little by little Bridgeton withered. One by one, the diners closed. The Jersey, the Lyric, the others—they're all gone. Angie, indomitable little Angie, remains.

"Sometimes you say the heck with it; you get that way sometimes," she says, sitting in one of her wooden booths. "But you just take it and go right along."

Her first husband died four years after their marriage. Her second husband died too. Angie goes right along.

A short-order cook makes breakfast on the grill out front; Angie does all the "heavy cooking" in the kitchen. Customers have followed Angie over the years, from the Cohansey Grill to the second Cohansey Grill to here.

Angie may outlive them all.

"Good Lord gives me energy," she says.

Every Saturday for forty-plus years, she's "run" chicken pot pie out on Saturdays.

"They pretty much eat what I put out," she says, allowing herself a smile.

How much longer will she keep working?

"I really don't know," she replies. "I hope I have the strength to keep doing it."

Then she gets up, excusing herself. Sorry, she says, there's work to be done.

◆ ◆ ◆ ♛ ◆ ◆ ◆

Tim De Filippis sells hash.

A-one, prime-quality hash.

"I like to sell the hash," he confides. "When I sell the hash, people think they're going to get what every other place has.

"It's real corned beef hash," he adds. "It doesn't come out like cat food."

Tim makes real hash, and real crab cakes, and a mean shrimp-and-scallop marinara, and a pot pie so good people reserve it in advance, and chicken soup with real stock ("not the gelatinous base you add water to and presto chango, you have soup"). He buys good Italian sausage from a guy in Vineland and tries to be the first one with fresh strawberry shortcake in the spring.

"When you're in one of these modern diners with a menu like an encyclopedia and you order chipped beef, it's not going to be fresh," he says. "Don't even try to tell me that."

The sports-theme interior of the Time Out Diner.

The Time Out Diner is located on a country road—Route 50, about halfway between Mays Landing and Sea Isle City—but people have had no trouble finding it since January 1990, when Tim and his wife, Belinda, opened the diner. They're among the new kids on the block in the diner world, men and women in their thirties who have left other—and usually more secure—jobs to open diners. Stan and Carol Kelley, who run the beautiful 54 Diner in Buena, are another example. Carol, a former casino cocktail waitress, and Stan, a heating and air-conditioning repairman, were about to leave for jobs in Cripple Creek, Colorado, when the diner became available.

The Time Out, a 1945 Silk City, had gone through several owners and names—most recently Rosie's—before Tim and Belinda took it over.

"Classic story," he explains. "Mother and father run it, mother and father pass away, daughters take it over, try to make a go of it."

The former Hot Cup Diner in Buena . . .

In 1989 Tim, a former 7-Up plant manager in Baltimore, who wanted to be his own boss, started thinking about the diner, which he knew from trips his parents would make from their home in Millville to Ocean City. Tom Tower, who owned the diner and property, was not interested in selling. Tim had one recourse.

"I sat in the parking lot for about ten minutes one day, came in, had a cup of coffee and asked [the diner's previous operator-manager], 'Hey, do you want to leave?'"

She did. The operation was his, for better or worse. He replaced the fixtures, the curtains, the shelves, the mustard-brown tables, the turquoise upholstery; added a grill, an ice machine, a steam table, and a preparation counter; and repainted the place inside and out.

"The kitchen was a mega-cleanup," he recalls not so affectionately. "Very dark and dingy. We did a lot of cleaning." He smiles. "Tons of Simple Green and Mr. Clean."

. . . is now the colorfully appointed 54 Diner, run by Carol and Stan Kelley.

Jukebox, 54 Diner, Buena.

It took him and Belinda four months to get the place ready.

"I picked January [to open] because I didn't know what I was doing," the thirty-five-year-old Mays Landing resident says, laughing. "I didn't even know how to poach eggs. I thought eggs were over or scrambled. Poached—what's that?"

That first summer the local economy "hit the skids."

"There were some days I'd go home with eighty dollars. I'd think, 'What the hell am I doing?'"

In 1990 and 1991 they lost money. In 1992 they broke even. In 1993 they "made a dent." Their best year sales-wise was 1994, but a higher overhead kept profits to a minimum.

"Ninety-three was our best year financially. People were waiting forty-five minutes to get in. You think, 'This is going to last forever,' but of course it doesn't."

His day begins about 5:30 A.M. and lasts until 10:00 P.M., when he goes home and tries to stay awake long enough to finish his vodka-and-tonic.

"My last day off was Easter, and I won't get another one until Labor Day, so when I flip everyone will know the reason why."

He is as tough on his help as he is on himself. Tim's rule: "You better cook it the way I want it or you won't cook it." What he wants in a waitress: "You've got to be smart and you've got to be fast."

Tim's heart is in the diner, but he's not sure how much longer his wallet can stay there. His daughter is almost two years old. He doesn't want to miss out on her growing up. A nine-to-five job—working for someone else—may be his only option.

"We are a success to a degree," he says. "We're alive after six years. We've established ourselves."

He figured that with the hours he worked, and the money he made, his salary last year came to "minus three cents an hour."

It was Friday night, and time for him to get back into the kitchen to make some shrimp-and-scallop marinara, or maybe some of the big fat burgers for which the Time Out is known.

"If you're going to do this diner thing," he says, "you might as well do it right."

Red Tower, Plainfield.

SHORT STACKS

*O*nce upon a time there were six brothers from Greece. (There were four sisters, too, but they don't figure in this story.) The six brothers came to this country in the fifties and opened a diner in the Bronx, around the corner from the Bronx Zoo, called the Six Brothers Diner.

"There was a brother there," Chris Karounos says, "at all times of the day."

In 1993 the brothers decided they needed a Jersey diner, so they looked around and found, on Route 46 in Little Falls, the Towers Diner, which had once been the Primrose Diner, the Ambrosia Diner, and West's Diner.

There were several other diners in the city called Six Brothers, so the six brothers from the Bronx called their new diner the Original Six Brothers Diner. Two of the six brothers—Brothers Five and Six—are involved in the Original Six Brothers Diner, and so are two sons and the wife of Brother Six, so maybe it should be called . . . oh, never mind.

Chris, son of owner Tony Karounos, graduated from Rutgers University with a premed degree and a minor in classical humanities but ended up working for his dad.

"When people hassle me about not being in school, I say, 'In the diner I can still wear whites.'"

◆ ◆ ◆ ♛ ◆ ◆ ◆

A diner in a shopping mall: how New Jersey. Bobby-Q's, run by the brother-and-sister team of Lisa and Bobby Howell, is in the Livingston Mall and yes, it's open for breakfast, before the mall opens.

A diner at the airport: how convenient. The Garden State Diner is a comforting sight for passengers in Terminal C (Continental) at Newark International Airport.

A diner in a schoolbus in an industrial section of Newark: how different.

Diner purists will say, "That's no diner, it doesn't have this, it doesn't have that," but it sure looks like a diner, with its diamond-plate stainless-steel skin.

"Expensive, but it's forever," says Wayne DeFrances.

He's the owner of the Curbside Cafe, which is parked in front of Ironbound Transport Park on Wilson Avenue, just down the road from Exit 15E of the New Jersey Turnpike.

Wayne bought the former Camden church bus ten years ago, worked on it here and there, and finally opened for business in the summer of 1995.

You can sit in one of the two booths—the bus seats are the chairs—or on one of the four Munchkin-like stools, bar stools sawed down to fit under the low counter.

This isn't one of those places where breakfast consists of things wrapped in plastic. You like cinnamon French toast? It's here. Chicken marsala? Real popular at lunch. Spaghetti with white clam sauce and garlic bread? Stop in on Friday.

"Yesterday was South Carolina, Minnesota this morning," Wayne says of the hometowns of his predominantly trucker clientele.

The cook/artist—he's done murals for businesses—would like to build another schoolbus diner some day.

"I looked my name up in one of those baby name books," he says. "You know what Wayne means? Wagonmaker. Maybe I'll have a chain of them someday."

Wayne DeFrances, owner of the church bus–turned–diner Curbside Cafe in Newark.

◆ ◆ ◆ ❧ ◆ ◆ ◆

"The people here are regular people," says Gil Ryan, eating a breakfast of eggs, hash browns, and toast at Angelo's Glassboro Diner. "You say good morning to a stranger, they'll say good morning back."

Angelo Tubertini opened a diner on this site in 1946. The current diner, a Kullman, dates to 1951. His daughter Mary Ann and her husband, Joe, now own it. Angelo died in 1980.

This is one of the most instantly likable diners in the state: small, lively, the grill right out front.

Angelo's Diner, a fixture on Main Street in Glassboro since 1946.

"It's good food, it's American food," Gil says.

The diner was once open twenty-four hours; then it stayed open until midnight; now it closes at 9 P.M.

"With what's going on out on the street," Joe says, looking down Main Street, "even the new restaurants close. Any business after ten is risky business."

"It's like a piece of the town," says Gil, an instructor in laser fiber optics at Camden County College. "There's a commonness here. I'd say it's the center of the community."

"Man, they dig this jive!" proclaimed a February 1956 newspaper ad. "If you have fast action spots, AMI's juke box is the one for you. It gives you the fast play, and record programming that keeps the jive-hungry crowd jumping . . . and spending!"

In the fifties there probably wasn't a diner around that didn't have a jukebox. Today the wall boxes familiar to that generation are hard to find; diners are more apt to have stand-alone units, or no music at all.

But up in Orange, Massachusetts, John Durfee keeps the classic jukebox tradition alive by stocking the world's largest supply of used jukebox parts.

"We have hundreds of thousands of loose parts," says Durfee, who works for Orange Trading Co.

How do those push-button jukeboxes work, anyway? All the wall boxes are hooked up to a master unit, usually in the basement. Each button on the wall box contains a designated number of pulses; when you insert your money and push a particular button—say, for "Rock Around the Clock"—the signal is sent to the master unit, which counts the pulses and selects the appropriate record.

◆ ◆ ◆ ♛ ◆ ◆ ◆

A good place to check out the classic interior of the Royal Diner on Route 22 in Branchburg is from the bar next door. You can see right through the window, although you might have to peer around the bottles of Jack Daniel's and Tanqueray.

"This bar was the original diner," says Ted Conklin, tending bar.

It was moved here in the late twenties by his father-in-law, Joseph Golack, who everyone called George. Then came a second diner, which was later moved to Route 78 near Clinton and called the Royal II. The current one is an O'Mahony from the fifties.

The Royal has a special place in my heart. I stopped there every weekday morning for seven years. My favorite waitress was Rose Valent. Rose wasn't as quick or energetic as the younger girls, but she was wiser, friendlier.

"You know who used to come in here?" Ted asks. "Buster Crabbe [1932 Olympic gold-medal swimmer and star of several Tarzan movies]. He used to come in here for breakfast and dinner.

"You go anywhere in the country, any truck stops, you'll bump into someone who knows the Royal," he adds. "I'm not bragging too much, am I?"

Summit Diner.

George Golack, who raised chickens and pigs on his Lebanon farm for the diner, died in 1987. His daughters helped out here over the years, but not anymore. For the first time in its history the diner is no longer in the Golack family. Nick Bouzo is the new owner.

"It was a good deal," Ted says of the sale of the several-acre property. "Real good deal."

"Ballpark figure?"

He hesitates, then says, "Under a million."

"Over five hundred thousand?"

"Over five hundred thousand."

Through the bar window we notice two people ordering lunch in the airy, spacious diner.

"They should do well here," Ted says of the new owners. "It's a good diner, a good location. That's the most important thing. Location, location, location."

◆ ◆ ◆ ♛ ◆ ◆ ◆

Food on the grill, Big Ernie's Diner, Wildwood: three regular pancakes, nine blueberry pancakes, one hamburger, eight slices of French toast, two orders of hash browns, two Reubens, two sticky buns cut in half.

Sounds like mid-morning, but it's two minutes past midnight.

"Always lubricate your grill," a spatula-wielding cook in his mid-thirties is saying. "If stuff sticks, you're in trouble."

A sign on the wall says:

6 MONTHS TO CHRISTMAS

61 DAYS TO LABOR DAY

SAVE YOUR MONEY

"They want a greasy cheeseburger, I give them a greasy cheeseburger," the cook says. "If the waitress comes back—'Can I get an omelette?'—I say, 'What color is their money?' If it's green, they can have anything they want."

The cook, Ernie Dieterle, is also the manager and soon-to-be owner. His father, Big

Ernie, bought the diner, formerly the Atlantic Diner, in 1982. Big Ernie is confined to a wheelchair due to an auto accident, but he's there to greet customers. His son runs the day-to-day operation—and plans for the future.

"I plan to kill the drop ceiling, hide the air-conditioning and heating units, glass-block the vestibule, expose the Formica [counter]," he says. "I don't feel we need a major restoration, just a little makeover. A little elbow grease and a hammer and we'll get her back to normal."

Big Ernie's Diner and the Wildwood Diner are just two blocks from each other, but there's plenty of business for both. Who's busier? Both Ernie and Jay Scrocca, the Wildwood's owner, say they have no idea. Big Ernie's, unlike the Wildwood, is open twenty-four hours.

"When my father bought the diner," says Ernie, "one of my first jobs was taking one of those spatulas and scraping the bubble gum from under the booths."

He peers into a simmering pot. *"Pasta e fagioli,"* he says, pronouncing it the Italian way—"pasta fazoole."

The key here is portion control and prepped foods. Two ounces of sauerkraut on each Reuben, two ounces of tomato sauce for the mozzarella sticks.

"Two key words I use are 'recycle' and 'reuse,'" he says, deftly splitting a club sandwich into four. "Tonight's potatoes, tomorrow's potato skins for $4.25. Leftover bacon, bacon omelettes; leftover sausage, sausage omelettes."

Leftover margarine wrappers are dipped into a hotpot; the drippings are used for melted butter. Nothing is wasted.

The diner is fifties heaven—45s, old cameras, and license plates decorate the walls and booths. There is etched-glass art of the usual suspects—Monroe, Dean, and Brando. Ernie thought the records were overkill and removed them, but customers complained, so he put them back. He'd like to bring Big Ernie's back to a true fifties diner—without the trappings.

"This was a mecca in the sixties," he says of Wildwood, which he believes has lost some of its luster. "People would come in, couldn't find a hotel, they'd give you money to sleep in your parking lot."

◆ ◆ ◆ ♔ ◆ ◆ ◆

The interior is near perfect: A white counter with red diamond-shaped tiles runs along the side; there are red curtains and stools, and stainless steel that absolutely glistens.

"During vacation, we clean, we take everything upside down, every corner," says Chris Elik, owner of the Bound Brook Diner.

His father, Steve, bought the Fodero diner in 1968; it had previously been in Cranford, according to Chris. The Eliks are from Macedonia; Steve came here in 1938.

"Everybody say, 'You've got to be Greek,'" Chris says. "I'm not Greek."

Bound Brook is a blue-collar town, the diner a blue-collar place.

"Prime rib, things like this, we don't do," Chris says in his low throaty voice. "Stuffed cabbage—people come from all over for that. Pork chops, steak. Excellent stew. Pot roast—we get calls on Saturday to save some. Most of the time we run out."

Tomorrow's specials: stuffed cabbage, veal cutlet, grilled sausage.

The Bound Brook Diner is also one of a handful of diners in the state without a regular phone—and, naturally, without a listing in the phone book. Chris says his brother removed the phone years ago to save money. The diner managed quite well without it.

You can call the diner, however, with a take-out order. How? By knowing the number of the pay phone inside. Other diners without regular phones? The Teamster's in Fairfield, and the Dumont Crystal. You won't find them listed in the phone book either.

The diner was handed down from father to son, but probably won't stay in the family when Chris retires. His daughter is not interested; his son died at the age of twenty-three. Many interested buyers have called Chris.

"I have a card somewhere from a guy in Texas," he says. "He said, 'Don't forget me.' He said, 'First thing you do when you decide to sell, you call me.'"

Let's hope that the stainless will shine forever, no matter where the diner ends up.

◆ ◆ ◆ ♛ ◆ ◆ ◆

"Why Miss America?" Tom Carlis asks. "The owner, he's coming from Germany, he's so happy to be here."

And that, Tom says, is how the Miss America Diner got its name.

Miss America, West Side Avenue, Jersey City. Best diner name in New Jersey. There are no first or second runners-up, either.

Phily Diner, Runnemede.

John Baeder, Bendix Diner,
oil on canvas, 1991.
(Courtesy of the artist)

John Baeder, Belvidere Diner.
(Courtesy of the artist)

Hackettstown Diner.
(Courtesy of Christine Guedon-DeConcini)

Ramoco Grill. (Courtesy of Marvin Krupnick)

Trent Diner, Trenton.
(Courtesy of Marvin Krupnick)

THE FIRST WEEK
THIS SILK CITY DINER
OPENED IT GROSSED OVER
$2800.!! AND CONTINUES
TO IMPROVE. NEW LOCATION
...GOOD FOOD...PROMPT
SERVICE...THAT DID IT...

Checker Diner, Somerville.
(Courtesy of Marvin Krupnick)

Turnabout Diner, Phillipsburg.
(Courtesy of Marvin Krupnick)

Silk City ad, Ackerman Diner, Emerson.
(Courtesy of Marvin Krupnick)

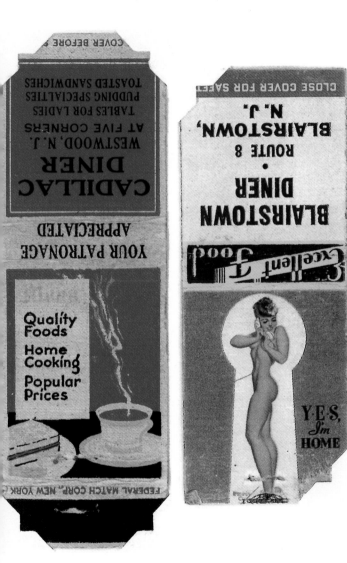

Cadillac, Blairstown, Scotty's, Madison Plaza diners. (Courtesy of Marvin Krupnick)

Rosie's, Diner World. (Courtesy of Fred Tiensivu)

Circle Diner, Raritan.
(From author's collection)

Fong's Garden, West Orange.
(From author's collection)

Steve Boksenbaum, Trucker, Triangle Diner, Folsom. (Courtesy of the artist)

There's no regular phone at the Bound Brook Diner, but if you know the number of the pay phone (left), you can call in an order.

It is an O'Mahony diner, built about 1945. The original owner was Fritz Welte. Tom and his partner, Sam Galatas, bought the diner five years ago. Tom had operated the Steak and Surf Restaurant in North Bergen; Sam had worked at the Skyway Diner in Kearny, which is where they met.

"Twenty-five years, I want to buy this diner," says Tom, who lives in Jersey City. "The German guy, he doesn't want to sell. Then I have opportunity."

He and Sam added new equipment, added a side dining room, spent fifty thousand dollars to renovate the kitchen, another eighteen thousand dollars to pave the parking lot.

"Is not working when I come," he says of the sign. "I fixed it."

Tom and Sam ("He is younger, more handsome") sound like good partners.

"I am tough, him is not tough," Tom says, smiling. "He is more, 'Anything good for the diner is okay, Tom.'"

The Miss America is "the Old Fashioned Diner with the Home Style Cooking," according to the menu.

"This is nice work," Tom says. "The thing is this. I come from the other side. I come illegal to this country [he is now an American citizen], I jump the boat. I work day and night at the beginning. I live for three years in the basement of friends. When I started I be dishwasher. Then I start to be grillman. This is the story of my life."

◆ ◆ ◆ ♛ ◆ ◆ ◆

A plate of pancakes in front of him to give him strength, a flu-weakened John Kourtis leans forward in a booth at the Rustic Mill Diner in Cranford to talk about his business.

Not the Rustic Mill, which he owns. His other business—saving fellow diner owners money.

"We felt that by getting together we would be able to fight them, or at least compete on an equal basis," says Kourtis, who looks like he is about to pitch forward into his pancakes.

Kourtis is president of Pan Gregorian Enterprises. Spend any time around New Jersey diner owners and you'll hear the term "Pan Gregorian." It is a cross between a co-op and lobbying group, a kind of Price Club for diner owners. Members pay an annual fee to Pan Gregorian, a corporation. Pan Gregorian strikes deals with the distributors and manufacturers that supply diners with everything from eggs and milk to dishes and napkins, and passes the savings along to members.

"We make a deal with the distributor, then members order on their own," Kourtis explains. "We buy eggs, for example. There is a newspaper that shows the market price for eggs. We have a deal with a distributor that says our price is four cents below the market."

Pan Gregorian has similar deals with fifteen distributors and suppliers, including AFI Foods, Bunzl U.S.A. Paper Goods, Pepsi-Cola, and Clinton Milk. Pan Gregorian makes money from its members, the members save money by buying at lower prices, and the distributors get more customers.

Whatever you do, don't refer to Pan Gregorian as a trade group or association.

"It is not association; it is corporation," the Rustic Mill's owner says.

Pan Gregorian was formed in 1983 by a half dozen diner owners. "There were other associations, but they were just to have dinner dances [and other events]," Kourtis explains. "We did not have control of the market. Everybody was charging what they wanted of the members. We got together to control the market."

Pan Gregorian doesn't have a motto, but if it did, it could be: "United we stand; divided we don't get a good price on bread and eggs."

There are now five Pan Gregorians: New Jersey, the largest, with about 250 members; Delaware Valley (South Jersey and Pennsylvania), with about 180 members; metro and upstate New York, with 100 members each; and Connecticut, with 110. Each is a separate corporation. Of New Jersey Pan Gregorian's 250 members, 200 are diners; the rest include restaurants, pizza places, and catering halls.

Somerset Diner, Easton Avenue, Somerset.

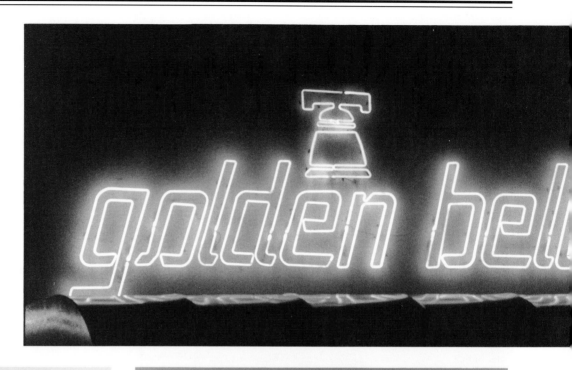

Right: Route 9, Freehold Township.

Below, right: Route 17, Paramus.

Below, left: The rock-solid exterior of the East Orange Diner.

Above, left: Hagler's Diner, Oradell.

Above, right: Route 511, West Milford.

Maxine and Rey Schmidt,
Time Out Diner, Tuckahoe.

SOUTH JERSEY LEGENDS

I sat down at the diner nearly everyone in South Jersey has visited at some point in their lives and ordered coffee and French toast.

The coffee came in a pot, something you see at too few diners.

The waiter wrote down the order and left the check in front of me, something you see at even fewer diners.

The French toast arrived—thick slices topped with powdered sugar—and I started to slice away. A waitress walked over, put her hands on her hips, and said, "Honey, where did you learn how to cut French toast? Here, let me show you."

She did, and then watched me practice-slice a few pieces, bringing the end of the knife more into play. She nodded her approval; I had passed the French toast test.

Now that, I thought, is a good waitress. Talks to customers who aren't even hers.

Several weeks later I told Tina George the story. She wasn't surprised by her waitress's behavior.

"People want service, quality, quantity, and attention—a lot of attention," she said.

Tina is the manager of Olga's. If you don't know Olga's, you don't know diners. Located on the Marlton Circle (the junction of Routes 70 and 73), Olga's is to South Jersey diners what the Tick-Tock is to North Jersey diners: institution; landmark; where the stars go if they want a late-night cup of coffee and piece of pie. Armand Assante was here once, and so was Liberace. You were expecting maybe Kevin Costner and Madonna?

The original Olga's Diner, Sixteenth and Federal, Camden, 1951. (Courtesy of Tina George and John Stavros)

"To Olga and her wonderful diner! With love, Liberace," reads the signed photo on display at Olga's.

"His hand was like cotton," John Stavros, Tina's brother, recalls. "I never met someone whose hands were that soft."

Olga and Tom Stavros, their parents, started a luncheonette called Mom and Pop's at Sixteenth and Federal streets in Camden in 1946. In 1951 they moved across the street to a larger space, which became Olga's Diner. In 1960 the current diner was built. The location seemed like a good one: There was talk of a new highway to the shore.

"When we came out here, nothing was here," John recalls. "The town [Evesham] didn't even have a traffic light."

"It was nothing but farm," Tina adds.

Olga died five years ago, at the age of eighty. But Tina is here, and so are her two nephews and John's daughter.

"To be honest," Tina says, "this is all I know."

In 1989 the diner made a cake for President Bush. It consisted of fifty-seven layers, and practically had a national security classification.

"You had the CIA in here," John insists. "I couldn't tell anyone about the cake; couldn't even tell my mother."

What does Tina look for in a waitress? Her answer is refreshingly honest.

"Someone who is interested in making money," she says. "That means she'll pay attention to the customer. She must be efficient—friendly and efficient.

"A lot of diners are real cold," she says later. "A lot of diners don't allow the waitresses to talk to the customers."

◆ ◆ ◆ ♕ ◆ ◆ ◆

Olga's is the queen of South Jersey diners, but there is another diner that is as much an institution in the lower half of the state. It's not as flashy as Olga's, and it's smaller. Both, coincidentally, opened the same year, 1946; both celebrated their fiftieth anniversaries in 1996.

The smaller diner, though, may have more history behind it or, at least, its owners are more conscious of its past.

"The original diner here was a nineteen twenty-eight or nineteen twenty-nine O'Mahony," says Burt Weed, sitting in a booth at the Club Diner. "It came with wooden wheels and a tongue in front to hook up teams of horses or a truck to pull it to whatever location was needed. They'd set up at a construction site, like a bridge or factory.

"They didn't have air conditioning [in the diner] then. The girls would almost pass out. You'd have to put a cold towel on them. When diners got air conditioning, they'd hang big blue banners out front."

"The summer I turned thirteen, I bused tables," said his daughter, Babe. "You had to work a lot harder then. We had to clean the windows—Mondays, Wednesdays, Fridays, this side; Tuesdays, Thursdays, and Saturdays, the other side."

Babe Weed: Now there's a diner name. Her real name is Carolyn, but everyone's called her Babe since she was—well—a babe.

219

CLUB DINER

"The food's always finer
At the Weed's Club Diner"

GOOD FOOD — GOOD PORTI

FAIR PRICES

Good place to stop

Morning, Noon and Night

Closed
memorial Day
4th of July
Labor Day
Thanksgiving Day
Xmas Day
New Years Day

3 SQUARES NORTH OF N. J. TURNPIKE ON ROUTE 168

BLACK HORSE PIKE   BELLMAWR, N. J.

OPEN WEEKDAYS 6 A. M. 'TIL 8 P. M. — CLOSED SUNDAY

Friday, Oct. 6th.

Juices	.15
Clam Chowder-crackers	.25-.30

Suggestions

Fried Egg Plant	.75
Fish Cake-2 Veg.	.75
Franks & Beans-1 Veg.	.85
Hard Boiled Egg Platter	.85
Salmon Cutlet	.90
Cheese or Western Omelette	1.00
Chicken Salad or Tuna Salad	1.00
Filet of Flounder	1.10
Deviled Crab Cake	1.10
Baked Halibut	1.25
Fried Scallops	1.25
Fried Shrimp	1.25
Fried Oysters	1.25
Breaded Veal Cutlet	1.25
Roast of Beef	1.40
Vir. Baked Ham	1.40
2 Gr. Pork Chops	1.75
Sirloin Steak & Onions	1.75

Choice of Two Vegetables

Mashed Potatoes	French Fries
Buttered Corn	Chef Salad
Buttered Limas	Pickled Beets
Baked Macaroni	Potato Salad
Stewed Tomatoes	Cole Slaw
Baked Beans	Cottage Cheese
Apple Sauce	Sliced Tomatoes

Desserts		**Beverages**	
Pudding	.25	Coffee	.10
Jello	.20	Tea	.10
Pie	.25	Sanka	.15
Pie ala mode	.40	Milk	.15
Ice Cream	.20-.35	Soda	.15
		Milkshake	.40

Virginia Baked Ham............1.75.

SORRY IF AT SOME TIME WE RUN OUT OF SOME ITEM LISTED
Side order of Home Fries - .30   Toss Salad-.45
Side order of French Fries - .30

Menu, Club Diner, 1940s.
(Courtesy of Babe Weed)

The Club Diner is located on the Black Horse Pike—Route 168, just off Exit 3 of the New Jersey Turnpike—in Bellmawr, Camden County.

On May 13, 1946, Burt Weed's parents, Ralph and Edna, opened the original Club Diner, once located in Hazelton, Pennsylvania. It stayed open until October 1972, when

Club Diner, Bellmawr, shortly after opening in May 1946. (Courtesy of Babe Weed)

the Weeds bought the former Somerdale Diner on White Horse Pike and moved it here. The original Club Diner, renovated several times over the years, ended up in Paulsboro; it is now the Cup and Saucer.

"In the thirties, diners were 99 percent men," Burt says. "Diners were for workingmen."

The thirties and forties brought emancipation, at least in diners. A 1946 photo shows the change. On one side of the diner is the message, A GOOD PLACE TO EAT, on the other, BOOTHS FOR LADIES.

Burt remembers that in the mid-1960s, waitresses working the counter would wear punch cards on their belts. Instead of writing down orders on checks, the waitresses would punch out item prices on their cards. It was up to them to remember who had ordered what.

"The food's always finer at the Weed's Club Diner," proclaims a mid-1960s menu. Coffee was fifteen cents; two eggs and toast, fifty-five cents; a hamburger, sixty-five cents; two grilled pork chops, $1.75.

In the 1950s each new waitress was given a copy of a training manual listing various dos and don'ts. "Don't put salt in the coffee!" says one caption. "If salt helped make a good cup of coffee, the coffee companies would be the first ones to add it."

The last few pages of the manual were reserved for personal grooming tips: "Use a good deodorant daily or several times a week according to your individual needs"; "If feet perspire, use an effective foot powder"; and "Insure personal sanitation by wearing clean under-garments."

The Club hasn't baked any presidential cakes like Olga's, but they did serve a vice president once—Dan Quayle.

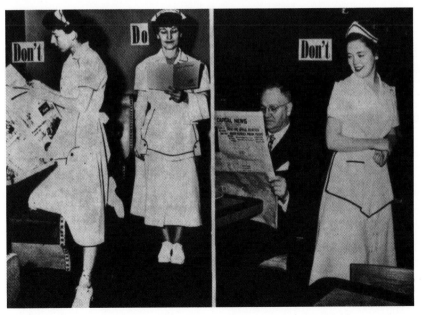

DON'T read the newspaper "on your station" or slouch in booth seats. DO study the menu. Maintain good poise at all times, even during slack periods.

DON'T read the customer's newspaper. This is no time to catch up on the funnies. The customer is ready to turn the page and wonders if you are, too.

Training manual given to waitresses at the Club Diner. (Courtesy of Babe Weed)

Cup and Saucer (the old Club Diner), Paulsboro.

The sense of tradition is strong here, with Babe running the diner her grandparents started, with the photos and menus she has carefully saved over the years. She looks at some of the new diners and doesn't like what she sees.

"Diners were diners," she explains. "What irritates me now is that people are renting a building, throwing the name up there, and calling themselves a diner when they have nothing to do with one. To me there's a little something special about diners."

Which is why you'll never see the Club undergo a fancy modernization—not while Babe is around, anyway.

What keeps her going?

"Going into the Cup and Saucer, feeling the legacy. Working with my grandparents and father. It's in my blood; I can't give it up. I would be letting them down.

"When I have problems that shake me up," she adds, "I pray to my grandmother to see me through."

◆ ◆ ◆ 👑 ◆ ◆ ◆

It is warm, cozy, and stainless-steel beautiful inside the diner on Mount Ephraim Avenue in Camden. Ferns and spider plants spill from pots attached to the ceiling. Waitresses—Lu, Henrietta, Ruth—dash in and out of the kitchen.

Three construction workers look over the book-length menu. Somebody orders a grilled cheese sandwich, somebody else the broiled fillet of flounder. A coconut cake beckons on a cake dish.

Wait, there's a smudge on the dish cover, and George Vallianos jumps out of his seat and dashes to the counter as if the diner were on fire.

He returns to the booth and sits down, but thirty seconds later he's up again, grabbing several menus and seating customers.

He comes back to the booth, only to get up and wipe something on the floor; sits down and talks for a minute or two before getting up to fill two glasses with water and deliver them to a table; starts to sit down, then goes away to turn up the heat.

"George," I say. "You have people who are paid to do these things!"

He starts to say something, but a waitress walks up and whispers, "George, can I see you in the kitchen for a minute?"

A diner never closes; a diner owner never sleeps.

Actually the 125-seat Elgin Diner in Camden does close at midnight every day, but if George Vallianos sleeps, it's probably not for long. This guy lives, breathes, probably dreams diners. He doesn't stop noticing things, doesn't stop fixing things, doesn't stop talking, doesn't stop period.

"Oftentimes I might take an order, grab a menu," he explains. "You have to."

The diner, with American and Chinese food on the menu, opened in 1958. Two years later it was in bankruptcy.

Jerry Vallianos, George's dad, who came to this country in the forties, started out as a dishwasher at the Garden State Restaurant in Camden—"a diner of sorts," George recalls, "an all-night, twenty-four-hour, you-can-see-the-kitchen type of place."

By 1954 Jerry was running Shorty's, a restaurant down the street from the Elgin,

George Vallianos, the always-on-the-move owner of the Elgin Diner.

then called the Fair-Lynne, after Fairview and Woodlynne, a section and adjoining borough, respectively, of Camden.

Jerry heard the Fair-Lynne was coming up in a bankruptcy sale and bought the Kullman diner. On Mother's Day 1961, Jerry and his brother, Spiro, opened the Elgin Diner. At the time George was twelve.

"I was a real meticulous guy," he says. "I told my dad to get a real good broom. My fun thing was to clean the parking lot. Not just clean it but clean the dirt off it."

But he and the Elgin Diner would not become inseparable until ten years later. George joined the Coast Guard, then the CIA. No, not that CIA, but the Culinary Institute of America (in Hyde Park, New York). He worked at several restaurants before ending up where it all began.

His uncle had retired from the Elgin, and his dad needed help.

"I really didn't know how bad the diner was doing," he says. "Generally speaking this place was running itself down."

The original Angelo's Diner, Glassboro.
(Courtesy of Mary Ann and Joe Justice)

Little by little he upgraded the place. Redesigned the menu, added new items. Replaced the "shrimp-colored red" booths and stools with burgundy-colored ones. Covered the blue and gold metallic panels outside with a thousand feet of vertical blinds cut to size by his dishwashers. Cost of that project: $276.

"We didn't modernize," he says. "We came back to the fifties."

The menu includes everything from Italian Hoagie and Pattie-Melt Hamburger to Breast of Chicken Cheese Steak and Golden-Fried Jumbo Shrimp with Crabmeat Filling.

Where did the name Elgin come from? George's father was sitting with his attorney one day when he noticed his watch. The brand name? Elgin.

"It could have been the Seiko Diner if it was today," George says, laughing.

More than 90 percent of diner owners are Greeks, but why? George explained his theory to writer Teri Dunn in the winter 1994–95 issue of *Roadside,* a lively, indispensable quarterly magazine published by Randy Garbin in Worcester, Massachusetts.

The diner, George says, has a cultural parallel back in the old country. Called a *kaffenion,* or coffee shop, it is a place to eat, drink, and gossip. The Greeks, he says, are not only food-obsessed but independent-minded, so when they immigrated to this country, many found jobs in the restaurant business, which was a natural.

And that, George says, is why there are so many Greeks in diners.

He markets the Elgin whenever and however he can. He gave out fifteen hundred calendars, printed five-dollar-off-a-meal coupons and mailed them to regular customers; took snapshots of those who attended a "brothers-and-sisters" promotion and displayed them up front; put take-out bakery price cards at each table because not everyone knew you could take those coconut cakes home.

It was twenty-nine years before the Elgin Diner got a newspaper food review, but that didn't seem to make any difference to the diner's loyal customers, who come for the food, the atmosphere, and waitresses named Henrietta and Lu.

"Where the hell else can you hear Harry James on the jukebox?" a regular asks.

George recognizes a familar face and gets up again.

"Hi, George, how are you?" the diner owner says. "Diet Pepsi large? Like a piece of lemon with it?"

LAST DINER TO CLARKSVILLE

The man with the deep, slow voice sits in his cubbyhole of an office, puffing on a cigarette, listening for a sound he hasn't heard much lately—the front door opening.

No one's in his little jewel of a diner, the one with red-upholstered booths, wooden coat hangers, a barrel ceiling so shiny it sparkles, and prices so reasonable you wonder why the place isn't always packed: two eggs with toast, $1.25; French toast, $2; grilled chicken breast, $3.25.

The stainless-steel vestibule, which reminds one of a space capsule, glimmers against the deep blue midwestern sky. Above the vintage clock are the cryptic words VASTA VERN.

"This property," reads a plaque on the yellow-and-red-striped diner, "is listed in the National Register of Historic Places."

Being one of only six diners on the register, however, is no guarantee anyone's going to eat there.

"In New Jersey everybody goes to diners—businessmen, bricklayers, college students," the man with the deep, slow voice is saying. "It just hasn't registered out here. This building might just as well have come from Mars."

Three years after opening the Clarksville Diner in Decorah, Iowa, Gordon Tindall had just about given up hope. He had rescued the diner from certain death, spent thousands of dollars repairing it, and now it was dying again and dragging him under in the process.

A few friendly reminders: Clarksville Diner.

The Clarksville's striking entrance. The
VASTA VERN *sign came from a*
South Jersey bar—Vasta's Tavern.

Gordon Tindall restored the Clarksville Diner to near perfection, but three years after opening, he was about ready to pack it in.

The 1939 Silk City diner once stood on the Penns Neck Circle on Route 1 outside Princeton, where it was known as the Princeton Grill. It had replaced an O'Mahony diner, the original Princeton Grill. In 1940 the O'Mahony was moved to a site on Route 1 North in Clarksville, where Quaker Bridge Mall is today. In 1951 the second Princeton Grill was moved to the same spot and renamed the Clarksville Diner, which is the one now in Decorah. One Princeton Grill had replaced the other.

Gordon, who grew up in Dutch Neck, would stop in the Princeton Grill on his way home from Princeton High School, but his destiny would not become linked to the diner's until many years later, and quite accidentally.

He flunked out of SUNY-Farmingdale and "knocked around for a while" out west, finishing school in California, where he didn't feel comfortable ("nine months of heat and three months of rain"). He ended up working on the railroad, the Milwaukee Road, as a track laborer.

He would cook for the guys in his crew, sometimes in campgrounds, sometimes in the caboose. They loved his spaghetti. He would get provolone, prosciutto, and *coppacolla* and make them real Italian subs.

His parents bought him a copy of *Gas, Food and Lodging,* John Baeder's paean to roadside Americana. Then his sister told him about a Pennsylvania diner called Uncle Wally's that was for sale. He suddenly decided he wanted to buy a diner. Uncle Wally's owner wanted too much money. He asked about the Melrose Diner, once on Route 130 in East Windsor.

"By the time we got around to that, it was gone, bulldozed over," he recalls.

He had heard the Clarksville Diner was spoken for—the property was being sold—but decided to give the developer a call anyway. If you can move it, he was told, it's yours.

Gordon was doing a lot of work in Decorah for Milwaukee Road, and the city seemed like a good place to relocate.

The diner reached town in April 1988. Gordon spent fifteen months dismantling it, piece by piece. He would take equipment on the road with him—polishing parts on one trip, repairing the stools on another. He stripped all the interior wood, added seventeen new windows and a retaining wall, dug out the basement.

A week before the Clarksville was scheduled to open in January 1992, a drunken driver plowed into it.

"He went right through the vestibule; he must have been doing fifty," Gordon says. "The clock shot up in the air and landed on the ground. There was metal and glass all over the place. The wall was all buckled in.

"I was numb. My wife was in tears. Some dumb guy stood in the doorway and said, 'Well, guess we won't have bacon and eggs tomorrow.' I had this hammer in my hand . . ." He pauses, as if afraid to say what he might have done. "What a stupid thing to say."

Gordon Tindall.

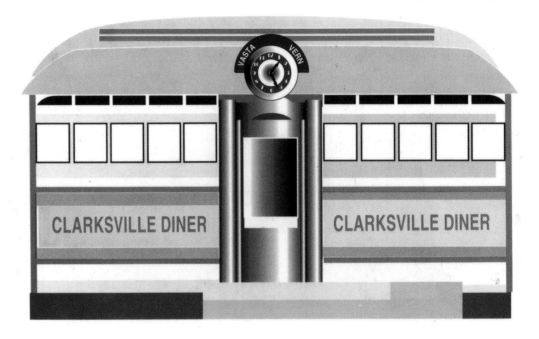

Clarksville Diner menu. (Courtesy of Gordon Tindall)

That night he called diner experts Dick Gutman and Larry Cultrera, who told him where he might find some abandoned diners for parts. The Clarksville's owner hopped into his car and drove east on a "treasure hunt."

He took the front door from the Pole Tavern Diner in New Jersey; the clock from the nearby Vasta Tavern; the vestibule from the Windmill Diner, near Harrisburg, Pennsylvania; stainless-steel bands from a diner in Berlin, New York. One diner was buried twenty-five feet underground (he didn't get any parts from that one).

He visited the Loraine Diner in South Brunswick on its final day of business and came away with two big sinks, a preparation table, a sandwich board and all sixteen stools, which he later sold to a woman who was restoring a diner in Rhode Island.

On June 16, 1992, four years after Gordon had it shipped to Decorah, the Clarksville Diner finally opened. The diner was "swamped" with business at first, even if Gordon's cook wasn't exactly working wonders in the kitchen.

"All the people who came here got an omelette that looked like the bottom of your shoe," he says, laughing.

He took over as cook, later hired one. When that one left, he became the cook for good.

"People rave about our soups," he says. "I don't think anyone in town makes it as good. People are always asking, 'What's the recipe?' I don't have any recipes; I don't remember what I put into it.

"We're kind of well known for our waffles. We use real maple syrup [from Green's Sugar Bush in Castalia, Iowa, according to the menu]. We're well known for our potato salad. I make it just like my mom did. Celery, sweet gherkins, hard-boiled eggs, onions, shredded carrots. Lot of places get a tub of that shit, with Miracle Whip and mustard, no pickles, no onions, heaven forbid there are onions.

"I've had customers say, 'I've never had potato salad like yours anywhere else in the world.'" He smiles. "If I don't have it for a day, they get all pissed off."

He makes the diner standards—eggs, French toast, grilled cheese, hamburgers, meatloaf. He also makes Reuben soup (corned beef, vegetables, Swiss cheese), shiitake mushroom curry, and jambalaya. He uses good garlic, shipped from California. Chili with chunks of beef, not hamburger.

He made the kind of subs he made for the guys on the railroad.

"We couldn't sell them," he says. "People go to Subway and spend three dollars for some piece-of-shit sub. Man, that sub was so good. . . ."

Business sucks.

"Every once in a while, the counter fills up, I'm so happy I can hardly contain myself," he says.

He's tried promotions, giveaways (free meals for kids if their parents sit at the counter), and advertising (a Hudson Hornet he pulled from a swamp in Kansas and restored appears in parades with the diner's name painted on the side).

"Another of my harebrained promotions that doesn't result in any new customers," he says.

He printed postcards and made up neat paper placemats on which kids could color in the six diners on the National Register of Historic Places, or design their own.

Zippo.

The Clarksville is one of six diners on the National Register of Historic Places, along with the Modern Diner in Pawtucket, R.I.; the Miss Bellows Falls in Bellows Falls, Vt.; Mickey's Diner in St. Paul, Minn.; the Village Diner in Red Hook, N.Y.; and the Tastee 29 Diner in Fairfax, Va.

Clarksville Diner.

"Our customers are fantastic customers," he says. "There just aren't enough of them."

Late in the summer of 1995, he had had enough. He put the Clarksville up for sale.

Then he reconsidered. While he was out mending a torn Achilles tendon, his former wife—the two had just divorced—ran the diner. She liked it so much she decided to stay on when Gordon returned. So he took the diner off the market.

"We're going to keep trying, not that business has picked up," he said later.

He still can't figure out why the Clarksville hasn't been a success.

"I don't belong to any country club, I don't go to bars, and I don't go to church," he says. "There are no roots here, even though we've lived here thirteen years.

"Maybe the people here thought we were entrepreneurs or something. But we were just working stiffs like anyone else, trying to make a living."

YOU OUGHT TO BE IN THE MOVIES

It's probably safe to say that John Diakakis is the only blind diner waiter in New Jersey.

"Blind since birth?" he is asked.

"Yes. Although in stand-up, I say it happened shortly after puberty."

Diakakis is not the only comedian in the Bendix Diner, but he's the only one who does it professionally.

"There's not a lot of money in stand-up comedy, and then you have bills that piled up in college," he says, explaining why he works the overnight shift at the Bendix Diner.

His dad, Tony, owns the diner, on Route 17 in Hasbrouck Heights. It's amazing that Route 17, which seems to have at least fifty of everything else—home electronic stores, fast-food restaurants, department stores, fashion outlets—has only seven diners.

The Bendix is the most famous of them. If you've turned on your TV in the past ten years, you've probably seen the Bendix.

The U.S. Healthcare commercial where Ray Charles is singing "America" on the soundtrack and the wedding party is running across a rain-slicked parking lot toward a diner? The Bendix. The Reebok commercial where the moms of pro basketball players Kenny Anderson and Sam Cassell are talking about their sons over breakfast? The Bendix. The Kellogg's Bran Flake commercial where one guy is eating a doughnut, the other bran flakes? The Bendix.

John Eliakostas, son-in-law of Bendix Diner owner Tony Diakakis.

A bowl of soup brings a smile to the face of a young customer at the Bendix Diner.

Tonka Toys, Coke, New Jersey Bell, Wisk, Maalox—the list goes on and on. All that atmosphere comes at a price, of course; John Eliakostas, Tony's son-in-law, wouldn't reveal how much the diner charges per commercial, but a safe guess would be five thousand dollars or more. The diner averages six commercials a year.

Movies shot in the Bendix include *Boys on the Side* and *Jersey Girl.* In one scene from *Jersey Girl,* Toby (Jami Gertz) has a falling-out with her friends, who accuse her of trying to act like someone she isn't to impress her well-to-do New York City boyfriend.

(COOKIE) I know you, and you are no longer you.

(TOBY) What the hell is that supposed to mean, huh?

(COOKIE, sarcastic) That means I drink Corona now. Hoops are out. Diamonds are in. Does that sound familiar? Tell her what it means, Ang.

(ANGIE) Dottie . . .

(DOT) Well, I guess it means if we didn't know you before we probably wouldn't like you now.

(TOBY) Why, because I don't hang out at the diner, is that why?

(COOKIE) No, it's because you look down on us now, like the city girls do. You are not from New York, Toby. You're just a Jersey girl trying to act like she's not.

(TOBY) Yeah, well, fine. Stay in your halter tops and your purple eyeshadow and your pink nails. Stay in Jersey because I don't give a fuck.

Tony Diakakis bought the diner, a 1947 Master, in 1985. He had operated several restaurants in New York City.

"My place in the Bronx, it started to get bad," he says. "Fights, you know. I stop here for breakfast all the time. I like the place. We ask the owners if they wanted to sell. They said okay. We closed the same day. They had an appointment with the real estate agent. I told them to cancel it."

Eight years ago he had a heart attack in the diner's kitchen.

"My wife [Eva] hold the place until I get better," he says.

Today his wife; his son John; his sister-in-law, Betsy; his son-in-law, John; and John's wife, Maria, all work at the diner, named after the Bendix Corporation, which made aircraft navigation equipment.

They definitely have fun. One Christmas, a trucker left John Diakakis a big bag behind the counter. In it were five thousand condoms and a note: "If finished in two weeks, I'll bring you some more."

John retaliated. Somehow he got hold of a goat's head and left it on the guy's truck.

The diner is a never-ending show, and at the Bendix, the customers provide much of the entertainment.

"We have one guy, he'll sit over on that stool," John Diakakis says. "He'll sometimes sit there five, six hours, with a newspaper and magnifying glass."

"I've never seen a guy eat fish like he does," Tony adds. "He picks it clean like a weasel."

"That guy, Don, he eats nothing but a bowl of spaghetti," John Eliakostas says. "No matter what time of day—two o'clock in the afternoon, seven o'clock in the morning. As soon as we see him coming, we put on the spaghetti."

"On Sunday, Monday nights, I'm the only one out here," John Diakakis says. "To be honest, I'm sort of amazed; I never thought I could do something like bring a cup of coffee to the table." He laughs. "Then I go home and bump into a wall."

How does he know when to stop pouring a cup of coffee? You can't stick your fingers in it, after all.

"By the sound," he explains. "It makes more of a hollow sound when it gets to the top. And you can put your finger on top and feel the vapor. I had to burn myself a few times at first."

His brother-in-law's dream is to buy an old diner and move it out west. The Bendix's owner, on the other hand, is not going anywhere. Tony says Jerry Berta, who bought New Jersey's most famous diner, Rosie's, and moved it to Michigan, has his eyes on the Bendix.

"He tells me, 'This is going to be my next diner.'" Tony shakes his head emphatically. "Not for sale. Never."

◆ ◆ ◆ ♛ ◆ ◆ ◆

On North Park Street in East Orange, where Orange, East Orange, West Orange, Glen Ridge, Montclair, and Bloomfield almost, amazingly, come together, is the Big Diner.

Or was, anyway. The diner lasted three days, then closed. To be replaced by the Harris Diner, which was there all along.

Whenever Tums wants you to feel guilty for stuffing yourself, it sends a production crew over to the Harris, scene of eight Tums commercials in the past two years. In one, a false front was built and the Harris became the Big Diner. Although a Harris menu is flashed briefly in the most recent Tums commercial, you can't tell it's the Harris unless

*Bill Nicholas, co-owner of the Harris Diner
in East Orange, location of all those Tums
commercials.*

you really know the place, but that's okay, because everybody, especially co-owner Bill Nicholas, loves to be on TV.

"They like it the first time, they call up again: 'You ready for another one?'" Bill says of Tums.

The Harris was selected from among dozens of diners screened by a location scout.

"It's a really great place," says Kate McLean, staff production manager at Porter/ McNamara Films, which shot the commercials. "[Tums] really loved the fifties look."

The food in the commercials didn't come from the Harris; it was prepared by a home economist. The production crew didn't eat at the diner, either; their food was catered.

The L-shaped diner, a 1951 O'Mahony, is one of the more striking diners anywhere, with its distinctive entrance and the word "Harris" in flowing script overhead,

Charlie Harris opened the Harris Diner in 1951.

the eighty-five-foot-long main dining area, and wooden floors behind the counter.

Charlie Harris was the original owner, with his wife, Mary. A story in the August 1957 issue of *Diner Drive-In* says Harris operated his own boats to bring in fresh fish. There was also mention of the diner's businessman's special: Navy bean or chicken noodle soup, Salisbury steak or baked mackerel, vegetable and potato, pudding or Jell-O, and beverage, all for eighty-five cents.

"In the seventies and eighties [local diners] went with the modern, and we stayed with the original," Bill says. "Everyone else has gone and we're still here."

Waitresses seem to like the diner, if not Bill.

"We've had waitresses who've been here thirty, thirty-five years," the sixty-one-year-old owner says. "If they're not here, they're dead."

"You must be a good boss."

"No, no. Listen to them. They tell you I holler too much in the kitchen."

He works 5 A.M.–3 P.M., while his partner, Bill Marmaras, works 3–10 P.M. The first Bill is known as "Little Bill," the second as "Big Bill."

"People say, 'You guys still together?' Anything we do, we do for the business. If it works, fine. Doesn't work, move on."

Move from here? No way.

"I have no intentions of selling the place, no intentions of retiring," he says. "We go from here . . ."

"To?"

He smiles. "Wherever, whatever."

◆ ◆ ◆ ♔ ◆ ◆ ◆

You'd expect the front of the Tunnel Diner's menu to show the Holland Tunnel, which is just down the street; or cars, thousands of which rush past the diner every day; or New York City, which those cars have just escaped.

No, the front of the menu features something more fitting: the Acropolis.

"There was a Jewish owner, a German owner, now we are two Greeks," says Steve Tsalavoutis.

For the past fifteen years, he and Mike Lignos have owned the Tunnel Diner in Jersey City, open since 1942. Several scenes in the movie *City Hall,* starring Al Pacino and Bridget Fonda, were shot here. The interior is well preserved, the exterior less so.

"The biggest mistake they make," Steve says of previous owners, "is this."

He walks around back to show the striking red and blue panels that once covered the diner. Today, the panels are hidden under the newer stone facade.

The food is hearty, filling. Steve is proud of his corned beef hash, mashed potatoes, grilled chicken, and jumbo hamburgers, to name a few. There is a printed menu, but the menu above the counter is the one to read. Among the items:

SPAHGETI

PASTRAM

WISS CHEES

DOUBLE CHEB

CHESBURG

EGG SALAT

"People like their food heavy," Steve explains. "Pot roast, short ribs, liver and onions. We have oxtail ragout, meatloaf. We make fresh veal cutlet. Nice bread pudding."

He thinks of something and smiles. "People say, 'The soup's good.' I say, 'You eat here, you die at home.'"

This particular week he is working eighteen-hour days ("Only Greeks work like this") because his partner is on vacation.

"You see we not try to be high-class place," Steve says later. "We try to be like family, like friend. Lot of places, waiter comes over, 'What you want?' I like to say, 'Come sit down, how are you doing, how are you feeling, you like menu?'"

He'd like to replace the booths, maybe add a back dining room, but everything else will remain, as long as he is here, anyway.

"From the outside it looks like old diner, but when people come inside, it is very nice. Some people like to look at new place. But if you have new place, you must have new prices."

The diner is on Boyle Plaza, the part of Route 78 that connects the tunnel exit to Route 1 and the New Jersey Turnpike. It is not a scenic stretch, but Steve tried to beautify it in his own small way. He planted sunflowers along the fence separating his lot from the adjacent gas station.

Someone promptly stole them.

◆ ◆ ◆ ♛ ◆ ◆ ◆

This scene from the movie City Hall *(1996), with Bridget Fonda and John Cusack, was shot in the Tunnel Diner in Jersey City.* (Courtesy of Castle Rock Entertainment)

Other Jersey diners in the movies:

Roadside Diner, Wall: *Baby, It's You.*
Raritan Diner, South Amboy (now in Ithaca, New York): *The Purple Rose of Cairo.*
Liberty View Diner, Jersey City: *Broadway Danny Rose.*
Teamster's Diner, Fairfield: *Angel Heart.*

◆ ◆ ◆ ♛ ◆ ◆ ◆

The script, titled "Baboon Heart," was written in a Hoboken diner by a guy who did stuntwork in *The Toxic Avenger,* which is why the eventual movie was shot in Minneapolis, attracted the interest of a rock megastar, starred Marisa Tomei and Christian Slater, and was retitled *Untamed Heart.*

Welcome to Hollywood.

"*Untamed Heart* opend up a lot of doors for me," says Tom Sierchio, who wrote the screenplay. "Madonna really wanted to do the movie; she campaigned for it. I went to its screening at the White House and met George Bush. And Chelsea Clinton requested it at her birthday party."

When the door your foot's in is connected to the White House, your career is probably headed in the right direction.

"They say write about what you know about," the screenwriter says. "I think the characters in this state are so much more rich than what I find in LA."

Which is why he does practically all of his writing in diners. Not just any diners—Jersey diners.

"I had basically my own table," he says of the Malibu Diner on Fourteenth Street in Hoboken, where he wrote much of his first ten scripts. "The waitresses called me 'writer.' They didn't know my name.

"Writing at home was too stifling, too quiet. A diner—there's movement all around but there's no distractions. And the dialogue you hear—you can't buy that."

Tom, a thirty-one-year-old with movie star—or at least movie screenwriter—

Tom Sierchio on location, Untamed Heart. *The Toms River resident wrote the screenplay.* (Courtesy of Tom Sierchio)

looks, sits in the Memory Lane Diner on Fischer Boulevard in Toms River, one of his favorite Jersey diners.

You look at his black leather jacket over white T-shirt, the waitresses' pink uniforms, listen to the diner jukebox ("Jailhouse Rock," "Charlie Brown," "Unchained Melody," and the like), and wonder whether you didn't slip down a hole somewhere.

Tom, a Bloomfield native, was a physical education major at Trenton State College "for about a day," he says.

"I had a volleyball class at eight A.M., said 'no way,'" he recalls, laughing. "I changed to speech and communication, and theater."

A friend introduced him to a stunt coordinator, which is how he ended up in *The*

Toxic Avenger. That led to stunt work in *Batteries Not Included, Last Exit to Brooklyn,* and other movies.

"I did a little bit of driving, but it was mostly high falls, stair falls, car crashes," he says.

But he wanted to write and direct, not just be a punching bag. Ensconced in his favorite booth at the Malibu, and later in the Toms River Diner and Memory Lane Diner, he wrote "Vineland," about a punk who befriends a resident of a retired actors' home; "A Soapbox Opera," a story set in Asbury Park about a quiet guy and a high-strung girl; and "Nocturne," a thriller about an insomniac who hasn't slept in eight months. In all his scripts he tries to set at least one scene in a diner.

He wrote ten scripts before selling his first one—"Baboon Heart." The movie, directed by Tony Bill, featured Tom in a small role as Marisa Tomei's blind date. His opening line: "My dad owns a hardware store. You ever need anything, just let me know."

Agnieszka Holland (*Washington Square; Europa, Europa*) is set to direct *Nocturne,* set in Hoboken. Ed Harris will star. Miramax is interested in "A Soapbox Opera." Tom will direct.

Life is good, but there's one problem. The Jersey native, who divides his time between the East and West Coasts, can't find a decent diner in LA.

"They have an excellent peppers-and-eggs sandwich here," Tom says of the Memory Lane. "You can't get that in LA."

LA's idea of a twenty-four-hour restaurant, he adds, is Denny's, which is why he always heads to the Memory Lane or the Malibu or the Four Star in Union City when he's back home. Atmosphere, characters, dialogue, unlimited refills of coffee—what more could a screenwriter ask?

"There was a guy at the Four Star—a leg breaker for the Mafia—sitting right behind me," he recalls of one visit. "This guy was straight out of Central Casting. He and his friends were talking about icing this guy, icing that guy."

Tom laughs. "He was complaining about how he was getting screwed out of his money. He did this one job, and they wouldn't pay him."

HAPPY WAITRESSES

he attractive middle-aged woman with the fiery red hair and tinted glasses looks around the little circular diner in Jersey City and smiles.

"I spent so many wonderful hours here," Joan Turino says.

She is sitting at a booth in the White Mana on Tonnele Avenue. At each window is a poinsettia in an aluminum-foil-wrapped pot. Except for the side dining room, little has changed at the White Mana since the late fifties, when Joan Turino worked as a carhop there.

"We spent so much time back there," she says of the diner's back room, "laughing and fooling and making plans."

The Mana's drive-in wasn't much, as drive-ins go. There were just lines, no barriers, no overhang. You'd pull in, and a waitress would come out and put a tray on your window.

"We worked out there until five in the morning," Joan says. "Union City was a lot different. You had a lot of clubs up there; they'd come down here afterwards. It was a different time, different element."

There were no uniforms; the girls wore slacks, with change belts around their waists.

"We had a fabulous business here," she recalls. "We're talking fifties, when people were hanging out, going to the movies. This place was hopping. Sometimes you couldn't find a parking spot here."

Joan Turino, former waitress at the White Mana in Jersey City.

Helen Melley, Miss America Diner, Jersey City.

We're talking fifties, when guys, at least those who hung around the Mana, talked about one thing more than anything else.

"Cars," Joan says. "Chevys were big. Guys would go down on County Road and race. They'd come back, look under their hoods, check things out. We'd call them the hoodlifters."

The girls could make a lot of money—one hundred dollars or more on a busy Friday or Saturday night.

"Some people would come down and order twenty burgers—murder burgers, they called them. I don't know what it meant; it was just a name."

The White Mana was not Joan's first job. That was in Union City, at a place where she learned how to win over customers: Before she worked at the White Mana, Joan was a burlesque performer.

Her friend Jim Murray, another White Mana regular, calls her a "stripper," but Joan says it was "family entertainment."

"It was a free-spirited time of my life," she says.

"When did you start dancing, in your twenties?"

"Oh my God, no," she replies, laughing. "I was fourteen. There were no child labor laws then."

She did an afternoon and evening show Monday through Friday, and four shows on Saturday at the Hudson Theater in Union City. Joan still has her burlesque outfits.

"They're gorgeous," she sighs.

She stopped dancing to work at the White Mana, then resumed dancing after she left the diner, but not for long.

"I went around the circuit once," she explains. "Cleveland, Canton, Toledo, Youngstown, Pittsburgh, Baltimore, Buffalo. . . . I didn't like the traveling. I missed everyone."

She sold real estate for thirteen years, then owned a bar in Hoboken for twelve. The name was appropriate: Redheads. She sold the bar two years ago; it is now called Scotland Yard.

A year ago she appeared as an extra in the movie *Into It,* starring Edward James Olmos. She played, of all things, a homeless woman.

"I wore this fabulous fake-fur coat that I had bought in Greenwich Village in the sixties, buttoned it all wrong," she says.

The White Mana's curb service was discontinued in the eighties. "People would take the tray, the food, everything, good-bye," says owner Mario Costa.

But the lady with the fiery red hair still remembers when the Mana was a hopping place.

"We'd always smell like hamburgers [at the end of the night], but we'd go out afterwards," she says. "It didn't stop us."

◆ ◆ ◆ 👑 ◆ ◆ ◆

The striking-looking waitress at the Colonial Diner in East Brunswick could be Joan Turino's daughter or younger sister. Same red hair, although the younger woman's is straight and long, not curly. Same free-spirited nature about her. While Joan Turino drives a convertible, Dee Kerekes rides a Harley.

Waitress Dee Kerekes with regular Keith Brown at the Colonial Diner in East Brunswick.

"Hi, Jimmie, how are you?" she says, greeting an elderly man at the counter. "Are those the glasses you're supposed to be wearing?"

Sometimes she's your big sister, sometimes she's your mother, but mostly a good waitress is your friend. You tell her things you wouldn't tell anybody else, and your secrets are safe. She asks about the wife and kids, knows when you're having a good day or a bad one, and, most important, she knows how you like your eggs.

"Doc, your bagel?" she asks a man who has just sat down at the counter.

"Everything, you know," Doc replies. "You know how I like it. Five years coming here, you know."

"Six years," she reminds him.

Dee started working in diners when she was ten, cooking, serving, mopping floors in the Woodbridge Diner, which her dad owned.

Debbie Simpkins, Salem Oak Diner.

Ursula Dylewicz and Wendy Stewart, Phily Diner, Runnemede.

"We were paid five dollars a week," she recalls. "That was good money. Sneakers [then] cost two ninety-nine."

Her dad was the original owner of the Clark White Diamond. Dee's mom worked as a carhop there; that's how she met her future husband. She told her daughter she'd make one hundred dollars in tips a day, and this was in the forties.

Dee's first real job was in the Silver Bell Diner in Lakewood. When that was sold, she came to work at the Silver Moon Diner, later known as the Blue Bay, on Route 18 in East Brunswick. That diner, too, was sold; she moved to the Queen Diner across the highway. And then the Queen was torn down for a highway widening. "Louie here [joked]: 'I don't know if I want to hire you, Dee.'"

Initially she worked just three days a week at the Colonial, which was all she wanted. Louie told her, "Dee, I have five days for you."

He knew a good waitress when he saw one. She started working 5 A.M.–2 P.M., the hours she works today.

"Good morning, Nick," she says to another regular. The cup of coffee and glass of water are on the counter before he sits down. "I was thinking of you last night. Those tomatoes you gave me were so good. Thank you."

When she started here, the waitresses wore mauve-and-green uniforms. "We looked like Braniff Airlines stewardesses," she recalls. She cut the sleeves off hers, and pretty soon all the waitresses wanted the same look. Dee is now the diner's unofficial seamstress; whenever one of the girls wants something done to her uniform, she takes it to Dee. Uniforms are not cheap, about seventy-five dollars for the pants, vest, and apron. She owns six of them.

"The smaller the size, the more it costs," the waitress explains. "The petite is harder to get."

A woman who has known Dee since the Queen Diner sits down.

"Muffins are good today," Dee tells her.

When she was out for a week with a sinus infection, customers sent her get-well cards. One Christmas a retired man gave her five dollars.

"He said, 'Dee, this is all I can give you.' That meant more to me than someone giving me one hundred dollars."

This is not a job for everyone. Sure the money's good, but your feet—and your future—can suffer.

JoAnn Russo, Colonial Diner, Lyndhurst.

Theresa O'Brien, Phily Diner.

"If a young girl asks me today about waitressing, I'll say, 'You can make good money but don't expect any benefits,'" she says. "You can work many years with nothing to show for it."

But if you're good, you never have to worry about being laid off.

"Who would ever think a waitress job would be more secure than a factory job or a construction job?" She laughs. "We don't have robot waitresses yet."

Robot waitresses don't ride Harleys. Dee waited a year to get hers, and has already ordered another one.

"Everyone has their escape," she explains. "That's mine."

In her spare time she teaches ballet and tap dancing: "I could never work one job. I'd be bored."

She's been a waitress for twenty-five years, and to her that sounds long enough.

"I think I'd like to be my own boss," she says, as the morning rush subsides. "I'm tired of working for everyone else. Years ago, when I had a little baby, I was afraid [to say that]." She smiles. "Now I'm getting gutsy."

DINER HIGHWAY

In New Jersey you can find diners everywhere, in every county, in half—284—of the state's 567 municipalities, on county highways and back roads, and even at shopping malls (Bobby Q's at Livingston Mall) and airports (Garden State Diner, Newark International Airport).

The first thing you see coming out of the Holland Tunnel (okay, so maybe it's the fourth) is a diner.

More than a quarter of New Jersey's 570 diners are located on ten of its major highways, among them Routes 1, 9, 22, 30, and 46.

Only one highway, though, can claim the title of Diner Highway. It's my second favorite Jersey road, next to Route 40, not because of all the diners but because it has managed for the most part to retain its rural atmosphere and escape the cancer of development that has fatally stricken nearby Route 1 and other highways.

Time to take a trip down—surprised?—Route 130.

The two diners we'll visit are at opposite ends of the highway—and of the diner universe. One seats three hundred people and looks like a cross between a pyramid and Egyptian tomb (maybe the pharaohs ate there?). The other seats about thirty and needs a new coat of paint. Each does its job extremely well.

◆ ◆ ◆ ♛ ◆ ◆ ◆

When Mike Fifis tells you that the inspiration for the imposing slanted facade of Ponzio's Brooklawn Diner came from a trip he took to Mexico, you think, Of course! It wasn't modeled after an Egyptian temple, it was modeled after a Mayan temple!

But the affable Fifis sets you straight.

"I was in Acapulco," he recalls. "I saw this dining room this way"—he holds a ruler up, slants the top down and away from him—"facing the ocean. I came back, told the architect about it."

The architect said, great, but it won't work. Too energy-inefficient. So the architect slanted the all-glass facade the other way, which would provide more floor, less ceiling—and lower heat bills.

"He talked me out of it," Mike says. "I'm very happy."

He and his brother Nick bought the diner in 1958. James Ponzio had opened it on October 27, 1949.

"He was called the King of Diners," says Alberta Lipsett, the diner's office manager, who has worked here since opening day. "He was an ace—immaculate, precise."

At the cash register downstairs is a 1949 newspaper ad announcing the opening of "Ponzio's Palatial Brooklawn Diner Restaurant." Ponzio had been director of the cafeteria and executive dining room at a Lipton plant in Hoboken.

"I remember those days," Alberta says. "Open all night. We had nineteen waitresses. I knew them all, their names, addresses, and phone numbers. Now they leave before I get to know their names."

Mike's first diner job was washing dishes at Nick Corcodilos's Hightstown Diner. Mike's brother once owned the Circle Diner outside Flemington. Asked what attracted him to Ponzio's back in the fifties, he replies, "Real estate."

Two years later he and his brother added ninety seats and extended the kitchen. In 1976 they built a new diner; the old Ponzio's is now the 295 Diner in Pedricktown. The new Ponzio's Brooklawn was built not by one of the established diner manufacturers (the original Ponzio's was a Kullman) but by Prince Co. in Pennsauken. Mike wanted high ceilings, but the diner companies couldn't accommodate him because the unit wouldn't fit under bridges along the way.

In 1965 he and Nick bought the Kingsway Diner on Route 70 in Cherry Hill and renamed it Ponzio's. A year later a new diner was built; in the seventies it was replaced with the current diner. The second Ponzio's Cherry Hill is now the Med Port Diner on Route 70 in Medford.

Nick retired and sold his shares in the Cherry Hill Ponzio's to his son, Chris, and younger brother, Jimmy. Mike now has what he calls a "small" partner in Ponzio's Brooklawn—Tony Moustakos.

If Route 130 is diner highway, Andros, off mainland Greece, has to be diner island. Mike and Nick, the Mastoris family, and several dozen other Jersey diner owners all come from Andros.

◆ ◆ ◆ ♛ ◆ ◆ ◆

At the other end of Route 130 is a weatherbeaten little diner that looks as if it would be a perfect movie set, although Hollywood hasn't yet come knocking on Chris Kokinos's door.

The imposing facade of Ponzio's Brooklawn Diner.

Liberty Diner, Route 130, North Brunswick: first stop on the Diner Highway.

Many diners are not open all night—the business is just not there—but they're always open at the crack of dawn.

If Max's Grill is the oldest diner in the state, the Liberty Diner in North Brunswick is not far behind. It opened in 1934—March 17, 1934, Chris says.

Back then Route 130 was a one-lane highway.

"No houses, no nothing," says Chris. "It was desert."

From 1947 to 1976 the Silk City diner was called Steve's Place. Chris came to this country in 1977—December 9, 1977, he says—and worked in various restaurants and diners, including the Colonial Diner in East Brunswick. During his first six months here, he slept at his brother's house.

"I start from the bottom," he says. "I worked dishwasher in the Colonial Diner. In the beginning it was hard. I didn't speak English.

"My first paycheck was a hundred and twenty-eight dollars for seventy hours. It was big money for me. That was my dream: to own a diner. I saved every penny."

In 1992 his dream came true.

"The people who used to own this place, two Greek guys, used to fight together," he recalls. "I stopped one day for coffee. I see ad in paper, 'Liberty Diner for sale.' I sit down over there. I said, 'Guys, if you're interested in selling, I would like to buy.'"

The deal was closed two weeks later.

While Mike Fifis can usually be found in his office, Chris Kokinos can always be found behind the grill. He's here at 5:00 A.M., leaves at 9:00 P.M. He looks in his fifties, but he's only forty-three.

"I don't know what a day off means," he says. "The only thing that matters to me is to make money to support my family."

He is dressed in the international diner cook ensemble—white shirt, white pants, white T-shirt, gold cross.

"I work and work and work, I work for my [three] kids," he says. "I want them to get education, something I never had."

Chris never got past the sixth grade, and yet he can speak four languages—English, Greek, Spanish, and some Arabic. One of his waitresses is Lebanese.

His wife, Elizabeth, works behind the cash register. They met on March 12, 1976; married May 2, 1976. Chris knows his dates.

"Everything homemade," he says of his food. "I make the soup; two, three specials each day. I don't think anyone else can beat my prices. My breakfast, nobody can beat it, my lunch and dinner, nobody can compare. I give you so much food."

His menu includes an item once found on most diner menus in New Jersey, but now on just a handful. We are talking, of course, about the happy waitress: grilled American cheese, bacon and tomato.

Here's Chris's theory on the name's origins:

"Long time way back, 1918, one of the owners of a diner in New Jersey used to go out with one of the waitresses. That waitress would come in very happy every morning. That's why he called [the sandwich] the Happy Waitress."

Like I said, it's a theory.

Chris Kokinos, owner of the Liberty Diner.
"I start from the bottom," says Chris, whose first job was as a dishwasher.

Route 130, Pennsauken.

Chris also makes the best bacon-and-egg sandwich in the state. In the Liberty Diner, that means big strips of bacon that stick out of either end of the roll.

"Sunday, between nine and ten [A.M.], it's going crazy here," he says. "I am going crazy in the kitchen."

Sunday afternoons, his only time off, he goes fishing.

There's plenty of competition nearby for the food dollar—seventeen restaurants, luncheonettes, and delis within a several-mile radius. What would happen if a McDonald's opened across the highway?

"Nothing, absolutely nothing. Anything, you could open there, it cannot hurt me. I am not afraid."

No one famous has stopped here, although Chris did meet Paul Newman once at the Edison Diner.

The Liberty, the last diner northbound on diner highway, could use a paint job, although Chris has planted flowers out front to liven it up a little. He also has a mango tree, which he takes inside in the winter.

"You work hard, one day you're going to be happy," he says. "Every day, I get up, come to life and I say, thank God, I made it another day."

The former Blue Pig Diner in Carneys Point, now a boardinghouse.

CLOSING TIME

The Excellent Diner's original owner was Louis Lekas.

*J*uly 30, 1995: Inside the diner people are shouting, laughing, taking pictures of one another. Harriet Frasiolas stands behind the cash register, shaking her head. Husband Steve, the cook, cracks an egg over the grill, a bemused look on his face.

A woman passes out song sheets and starts to sing—to the tune of "Carolina in the Morning"—this makeshift song:

> Nothin' could be finer than to meet ya at the diner in the mornin'
> Nothin' could be sweeter than the way Steve'll greet you in the mornin'
> When she takes your orders
> Harriet does great
> Steve will cook such wonders
> You'll want to fill your plate

Waitress Lisa Gutmann—self-described "beverage chick"—walks over to regulars Terry and Ken Wooster and asks happily, "What will you do without me?"

Behind them someone pops the cork of a bottle of champagne. The atmosphere is remarkably jolly—for a funeral.

July 30, 1995. A day that for thousands of people will forever live in diner infamy.

The Excellent Diner, for nearly fifty years more of a town hall than Westfield's own town hall, is closing for good.

"People are asking us for autographs," Harriet says. "I can't believe it."

The diner, built by Jerry O'Mahony Inc. of Elizabeth ("In our line, we lead the world," says a plaque above the door), opened in 1948. The original owner was Louis Lekas. Twenty years ago he sold the diner to the Frasiolases, she a former waitress, he a former cook who had met while she was working in the Edison Diner.

But the Lekas family held on to the 23-by-100-foot lot. The Frasiolases' twenty-year-lease expired in 1995, and they couldn't work out an agreement with Lekas's widow, Stella. When Bernd Richter heard the news, he quickly made an offer and bought the diner for sixty thousand dollars.

The Excellent Diner is now in Aalen, Germany, 100 miles from Munich; Richter, a German businessman who owns a company called Oldies but Goodies, wants to import other American diners to Germany, hoping to duplicate the success of the Fat Boy chain, all former American diners, in London.

*Baby photos, and a stern message,
decorated the register.*

Steve, in a pensive mood.

American diners are a hot item in Europe; the former Beach Haven Diner is now Reggie's Diner, in Barcelona, Spain. Owner Reggie Lock also bought the Flash-in-the-Pan Diner, once of Danvers, Massachusetts, and moved it to Madrid. He, too, would like to get his hands on as many American diners as he can.

"Come and visit the Excellent Diner in Aalen," read a sign on the window on the diner's last day. "Have breakfast with us for free. We look forward to serving you! The new owners."

It was a nice gesture, but it didn't make things any easier inside the Excellent.

"If you were going to lose one place in town, this would be the last place you'd want to lose," said Tom Murtishaw of Westfield. "Everything else is so sterile."

Beside him sat his four-year-old daughter, Taylor, enjoying her favorite Excellent Diner meal: one pancake and a glass of chocolate milk.

"Her mother will kill me for giving her pancakes for lunch," Murtishaw said, smiling, "but it's the last time."

Steve was on the grill making the last meals in the diner's history, or at least its history in this country. Harriet's mom, Bess Cohen, and daughter, Melissa, took orders, along with Lisa Gutmann. The diehards were there—Frank Tabor in the last booth, Ken and Terry Wooster in a booth up front, Fred Nurman in his usual place in the diner during the past fifteen years—second stool from the end, against the window.

"The day," he said quietly, "has come."

"There's so many people from here I know to say hello to, even though I don't know their last names," said Ken Wooster, a Fuller Brush distributor and a regular here for fifteen years.

Last supper—or lunch, anyway—for a couple of youthful regulars.

The Excellent's counter, an hour after the diner closed for good.

Harriet Frasiolas hugs a loyal customer on the last day.

"I feel like we let them down," said Natalie Ross Miller. "I feel like we should picket somebody."

But the sale happened so quickly there was little time for an outcry. In any case, none ever came.

Miller, a Westfield actress who plays "rich bitch" Enid Nelson on the soap opera *All My Children,* led another rendition of "Carolina in the Morning":

> Nothing could be greater than the smell of fried potatoes in the mornin'
> Bess and Sydney, Denny, Stevie, Darryl or Melissa say good mornin'
> Steve will say he's lousy
> But he isn't grouchy
> Long as you pay your dough
> Bring us back our diner 'cause we can't find nothin' finer in the mornin'

For the last day, a Sunday, Nurman brought a cake, someone else a bottle of champagne.

"I've eaten at a lot of diners, but this one has the homey, almost Andy Griffith, catch-up-on-news atmosphere about it," Nurman explained. "I live alone and have diabetes. If I'm not here two days in a row, they call me at home to make sure everything is okay."

"They make you feel at home," Tabor said of the Frasiolases. "Lot of diners, you sit there, they take your order, that's all they say to you."

At the Excellent regulars were allowed to get their own coffee. Three commercials were shot here, for Macy's, Trident gum, and the *Cleveland Plain Dealer.* The producer on the last shoot knew a good location when she saw one; she was from Westfield.

Several Columbia University students shot a movie here once.

"It's about these two guys," Harriet recalled. "They're trying to kill somebody, or they're trying to con somebody, and the con gets conned." She smiled. "It was cute." She never saw the movie, which may have been for the best.

"One of our customers," Steve said, "brought a brand-new baby here straight from the hospital to show everyone." Pause. "The baby had double eggs and sausage."

"People have been snapping pictures for the past week and a half," Harriet said on the diner's last day. "I'm not photogenic. In person I'm bad enough. In pictures I'm even worse."

"Lousy," Steve Frasiolas would reply when someone asked him how he was doing, so a longtime customer gave him this T-shirt as a going-away present.

Taped to the cash register, along with snapshots of various babies, was a red plaque that read: "According to the gospel of Harriet: All friendships end right here!"

Behind the counter were presents from well-wishers: perfume for Harriet; a T-shirt for Steve that bore the motto *Lousy,* which was what he always said when asked how he was doing; several Swiss Army knives (Harriet couldn't figure out why); and dozens of lottery tickets, several with the number 730—the diner's last day.

"There was a man in here last week who just broke down and cried," Harriet said.

They planned to take off a month and look for another diner to run.

A sign near this one on the final day carried a message from the diner's new owner. It promised a free breakfast to any Excellent patron who stopped at its new location—in Aalen, Germany.

"We want small," Harriet said. "We want enough to pay the bills. We're not greedy."

A local restaurant owner walked in and handed Harriet an envelope. Inside was a gift certificate: dinner for two at his place.

Shortly after 3:00 P.M., Steve cooked his last order at the Excellent Diner: two onion-and-cheese omelettes. "That's it," he said. "Who wants my apron?"

Someone grabbed it immediately.

A customer walked to the counter and paid her bill.

"Thank you," she said, hugging Harriet.

"It's been a pleasure," the owner replied.

"I don't know where I'll go now," Frank Tabor said on his way out the door. "Probably my wife's cooking."

"As soon as she heard it was moving," Tom Murtishaw said of his four-year-old daughter, "she asked, 'How can we get to Germany?'"

On the counter was a loose-leaf notebook; Steve and Harriet had promised to let those who wrote down their names and addresses know where they ended up. By closing time, there were 628 names. Many wrote down comments:

No one makes a better Yankee bean soup than the Excellent. Emily Tell, Westfield.

Steve: Nobody does a poached egg like you do. Irene, Scotch Plains.

Sorry, but I can't write very well. If I could I'd say something about how nice it was coming here. Best of luck. Love, Michael S. "Popcorn" Goldberger.

We're not eating until you call. Roger and Meredith Brody, Watchung.

NEW JERSEY DINER DIRECTORY

The following listing is accurate as of press time, but keep in mind that diners do change locations and telephone numbers. Diners without phone numbers are currently vacant or undergoing renovation/change of ownership. The directory includes authentic diners now operating as ethnic restaurants, pizzerias, or other businesses. Like the rest of the book, it is copyrighted; information from this list may not be duplicated without permission of the author.

◆ ◆ ◆ 👑 ◆ ◆ ◆

ABBIE'S DINER
300 Sicomac Ave., Wyckoff
201–847–0336

ABERDEEN DINER
1077-G Rte. 34, Aberdeen
732–583–2100

ADELPHI RESTAURANT & DINER
Rte. 35 North, Hazlet
732–335–9360

AIRPORT DINER
2602 Bay Ave., Ocean City
609–399–3663

ALEXIS DINER
3130 Rte. 10, Denville
973–361–8000

ALL SEASONS DINER
176 Wyckoff Rd., Eatontown
732–542–9462

ALL STAR DINER
17 E. Clinton St., Newton
973–579–2287

AL'S DINER
869 Communipaw Ave., Jersey City
201–434–5055

AMERICANA DINER
475 Rte. 46, Belvidere
908–475–3144

AMERICANA DINER
Rte. 130 North, East Windsor
609–448–4477

AMERICANA DINER
Rte. 35 and Shrewsbury Ave., Shrewsbury
732–542–1658

AMWELL VALLEY DINER RESTAURANT
Rte. 31, Ringoes
609–466–2030

ANABEL #2
424 Harrison Ave., Harrison
973–482–0058

ANAPA'S COUNTRY HOUSE
122 S. Pemberton Rd., Pemberton
856–894–2700

ANDERSON DINER
703 Anderson Ave., Cliffside Park
201–941–4808

ANDOVER DINER
Rte. 206, Andover
973–786–6641

ANDROS DINER
6 Wilson Ave., Newark
973–344–8415

ANGELO'S GLASSBORO DINER
26 N. Main St., Glassboro
856–881–9854

ANN'S DINER
323 Division St., Elizabeth
908–353–9747

APOLLO DINER
Rte. 33, Collingwood Park
732–938–4567

APOLLO DINER & RESTAURANT
101 E. Andrews Ave., Wildwood
609–522–0909

ARENA DINER RESTAURANT
250 Essex St., Hackensack
201–342–2275

ARLINGTON DINER
1 River Rd., North Arlington
201–998–6262

ARMETA'S RESTAURANT
5–7 S. Munn Ave., Newark
973–371–3436

ATHENA'S FAMILY RESTAURANT
1515 New Rd., Northfield
609–641–5725

ATLANTIC HIGHLANDS DINER
77 First Ave., Atlantic Highlands
732–291–1005

BAND WAGON DINER
2501 Rte. 37, Toms River
732–270–6400

BARNEGAT DINER
849 W. Bay Ave., Barnegat
609–607–8566

BAXTER'S SOUTHERN DINER
1332 E. State St., Trenton
609–689–1609

BAYONNE DINER
226 Broadway, Bayonne
201–823–8416

BAYSIDE DINER
2404 S. Bay Ave., Beach Haven
609–492–5202

BAYVILLE DINER
456 Atlantic City Blvd., Bayville
732–269–9860

BAYWAY DINER
2019 S. Wood Ave., Linden

BEACH HOUSE DINER
121 Atlantic City Blvd., Bayville
732–557–0050

BENDIX DINER
Rte. 17 and Williams Ave., Hasbrouck Heights
201–288–0143

BERKSHIRE DINER
7024 Bergenline Ave., North Bergen
201–869–0617

BERLIN DINER
117 S. White Horse Pike, Berlin
856–753–7474

BLAIRSTOWN DINER
186 Rte. 94, Blairstown
973–362–6070

BLUE DIAMOND
Rte. 575, Pomona

BLUE MOON DINER
1 Sloan St., South Orange
973–761–6666

BLUE PLANET DINER
841 Asbury Ave., Ocean City
609–525–9999

BLUE SWAN DINER
2116 Rte. 35 South, Oakhurst
732–493–2424

BOMBAY DINER
1303 Prince Rodgers Ave., Bridgewater
908–575–8060

BOONTON DINER
909 Main St., Boonton
973–263–9736

BRIDGETON GRILLE
1½ E. Broad St., Bridgeton
856–451–0220

BRIDGEWATER DINER
1244 Rte. 22, Bridgewater
908–725–8118

BRIDGE-WAY DINER & RESTAURANT
Rte. 9, Old Bridge
732–679–1599

BROADWAY DINER
1081 Broadway, Bayonne
201–437–7338

BROADWAY DINER
45 Monmouth St., Red Bank
732–224–1234

BROADWAY DINER
55 River Rd., Summit
908–273–4353

BROOKLAWN DINER & RESTAURANT
Rte. 130, Brooklawn
856–742–0035

BROOKS DINER RESTAURANT
Rte. 46, Pine Brook
973–575–3200

BROOKSIDE DINER & RESTAURANT
Rte. 10 East, Whippany
973–515–4433

BROWNS MILLS FAMILY DINER
RESTAURANT
127 Trenton Rd., Browns Mills
856–893–5500

BROWNSTONE DINER &
PANCAKE FACTORY
426 Jersey Ave., Jersey City
201–433–0471

BUDD LAKE DINER
100 Rte. 46, Budd Lake
973–691–9100

BURLINGTON DINER/AMY'S
OMELETTE HOUSE
Rte. 130 and High St., Burlington
609–386–4800

BUTLER FAMILY RESTAURANT & DINER
134 Main St., Butler
973–838–6690

BYRAM DINER
Rte. 206, Byram
973–347–5250

CAFE EVEREST DINER
2002 Park Ave., South Plainfield
908–755–2811

CALDWELL DINER
332 Bloomfield Ave., Caldwell
973–228–2855

CANDLEWYCK DINER
179 Paterson Ave., East Rutherford
201–933–4446

CAPITOL DINER/MARGHERITA'S
1044 Broad St., Newark
973–622–4224

CAPTAIN JOHN'S
Long Beach Blvd. and 20th St., Surf City
609–494–0924

CASTLE DINER
Rte. 33, Neptune Township
732–922–8419

CAVALIER RESTAURANT DINER
2401 Wood Ave., Roselle
908–241–8386

CEDAR LANE GRILLE
749 Cedar Lane, Teaneck
201–836–2837

CHANGE KARATE
Rte. 130 North and Church Rd., Cinnaminson

CHERRY HILL COACH DINER
Rte. 38 and Cooper Landing Rd., Cherry Hill
856–667–8255

CHERRY TREE DINER
806 Haddonfield Rd., Cherry Hill
856–488–2224

CHESTER HILLS DINER
65 Rte. 206, Chester
908–879–7423

CHINATOWN DINER
600 Broad St., Newark
973–596–1888

CLEMENTINE'S DINER
18 Boulevard, Seaside Heights
732–854–0900

CLINTON STATION DINER
2 Bank St., Union Township (Hunterdon County)
908–713–0012

CLUB DINER
20 N. Black Horse Pike, Bellmawr
856–931–2880

COACH HOUSE DINER
921 Kennedy Blvd., North Bergen
201–864–8600

COACH HOUSE RESTAURANT & DINER
Rte. 4, Hackensack
201–488–4999

COBBLESTONE DINER RESTAURANT
78 Rte. 35, Eatontown
732–542–4488

COLLINGSWOOD DINER
201 Crescent Blvd., Collingswood
856–858–8461

COLONETTE RESTAURANT
405 Rte. 440, Jersey City
201–432–8222

COLONIAL DINER
560 Rte. 18, East Brunswick
732–254–4858

COLONIAL DINER
27 Orient Way, Lyndhurst
201–935–3192

COLONIAL DINER & RESTAURANT
429 Lacey Rd., Forked River
609–971–2627

COLONIAL DINER RESTAURANT
924 N. Broad St., Woodbury
856–848–6732

COLOSSEUM DINER
1932 St. Georges Ave., Linden
908–925–2777

CONLON'S DINER
1807 45th St., North Bergen
201–866–4554

COOKSTOWN DINER
New Egypt–Cookstown Rd., Cookstown
609–758–7749

COPPER KETTLE RESTAURANT DINER
Rte. 9 North, Lakewood
732–370–9282

CORNER POST DINER & RESTAURANT
Brick Mall, Rte. 549, Brick
732–920–1337

COUNTRY CLUB DINER & RESTAURANT
Haddonfield-Berlin Rd., Voorhees
856–428–7462

COUNTRY DINER
40–18 Broadway, Fair Lawn
201–796–9796

COUNTY LINE DINER
2010 W. County Line Rd., Jackson
732–370–8740

COURT HOUSE DINER FAMILY
RESTAURANT
218 Stone Harbor Blvd., Cape May Court House
609–465–8008

CRANFORD RESTAURANT DINER
7 North Ave., Cranford
908–272–2800

CRESTWOOD DINER & RESTAURANT
Cresse and New Jersey aves., Wildwood
609–522–3392

CROSSROADS DINER
Rte. 46, White Township
908–475–2577

CROWN POINT DINER
821 Crown Point Rd., Westville
856–742–0880

CRYSTAL DINER
2009 Brunswick Ave., Lawrenceville
609–392–3500

CRYSTAL DINER
Rte. 37 West, Toms River
732–244–6262

CRYSTAL LAKE DINER
572 Cuthbert Blvd., Haddon Township
856–854–1965

CRYSTAL PALACE
1601 County Line Rd., Lakewood
732–364–7272

CUTTING BOARD DELI & GRILL
1275 Bloomfield Ave., Fairfield
973–244–5771

DAVIS DINER
135 Bond St., Bridgewater
908–725–7323

DEEPWATER DINER
455 Shell Rd., Carneys Point
856–299–1411

DELUCA'S DINER PIZZA & PASTA HOUSE
9407 Ventnor Ave., Margate
609–823–2988

DENVILLE DINER
17 Broadway, Denville
973–625–3133

DEPOT DINER EXPRESS
373 Rte. 9, Woodbridge
732–634–8989

DETROIT DINER
204 Martin Luther King Dr., Jersey City
201–432–3377

DIAMOND DINER
6711 W. Washington Ave., Cardiff
609–646–6656

DIAMOND DINER RESTAURANT
Rte. 73, Voorhees
856–424–8585

DIAMOND SPRING DINER
23 Diamond Spring Rd., Denville
973–627–6607

DIMPLES DINER & FAMILY RESTAURANT
Lacey Rd., Manchester
732–350–3030

DINER EXPRESS
47 Washington St., Morristown
973–605–5222

DINIC'S BEEF & PORK
Black Horse Pike and Kings Hwy., Mount
Ephraim
856–931–6328

DINO'S SEAVILLE DINER
33 Rte. 50, Seaville
609–624–3100

DON'S DINER
667 Nye Ave., Irvington
973–373–3055

DOO WOP DINER
4010 Boardwalk, Wildwood
609–522–7880

DOSA DINER
72 Broadway, Passaic
973–470–8181

DOT & TOM'S DINER
Wilson Ave., west of Avenue P, Newark

DOUBLE S DINER
Rte. 23 South, Hamburg
973–875–8419

DOVER DINER
Rte. 166, Toms River
732–349–3060

DOWN NECK DINER
671 Market St., Newark
973–344–6565

DUCHESS DINER
338 Lake Ave., Metuchen
732–548–5393

DUMONT CRYSTAL DINER
45 W. Madison Ave., Dumont
201–387–1212

DYNASTY DINER
117 E. Main St., Tuckerton
609–296–7227

EAGLE ROCK DINER & RESTAURANT
410 Eagle Rock Ave., West Orange
973–325–9057

EAGLES NEST DINER
4 Hamburg Ave., Sussex
973–702–8763

EAST ORANGE DINER
431 Main St., East Orange
973–672–7390

ECHO QUEEN DINER
Rte. 22 East, Mountainside
732–233–1098

EDGEWATER QUEEN DINER
4207 Rte. 130 South, Edgewater Park
856–871–5228

EDISON DINER
Rte. 1 South, Edison
732–985–3335

EGG PLATTER DINER
159 Crooks Ave., Paterson
973–684–3291

ELENI'S PANCAKE HOUSE & FAMILY
RESTAURANT
15 Grand Ave., Montvale
201–666–8651

ELGIN DINER
2621 Mt. Ephraim Ave., Camden
856–962–7155

ELMA'S DINER & BARBECUE
500 Watchung Ave., Plainfield
908–668–9898

ELMER DINER
4915 Harding Hwy., Elmer
856–358–3600

ELMWOOD PARK DINER
375 Market St., Elmwood Park
201–796–6641

EL SAZON GRILL
246 Grand St., Paterson
973–881–8288

EMPIRE DINER
1315 Rte. 46 East, Parsippany
973–335–2729

EMPRESS RESTAURANT
Fair Lawn Ave. and River Rd., Fair Lawn
201–791–2895

ENGLEWOOD DINER
54 Engle St., Englewood
201–569–8855

ESQUIRE DINER
Rte. 206, Springfield Township
856–267–6544

EWING DINER
1099 Parkway Ave., Ewing
609–882–5519

FAIRMOUNT DINER
641 Main St., Hackensack
201–489–2135

FAT BOY SUBS
143 Main St., Madison
973–377–3959

55TH STREET DINER
7 55th St., Ocean City
609–391–9292

54 DINER
Rte. 54 South, Buena
856–697–6116

FIVE POINTS DINER RESTAURANT
Rtes. 41 and 47, Deptford
856–228–5166

FIVE STAR DINER
Rte. 206 North, Branchville
973–948–2611

FLANDERS DINER
286 Rte. 206, Flanders
973–584–0007

FLEMINGTON FAMILY RESTAURANT
275 Rte. 202/31, Raritan Township
908–788–7882

FORKED RIVER DINER
Rte. 9, Forked River
609–693–2222

FORT LEE PIZZERIA
2469 Lemoine Ave., Fort Lee
201–947–2420

FORUM RESTAURANT
211 Rte. 4, Paramus
201–845–8850

FOUNTAINBLEAU DINER
1052 Stelton Rd., Piscataway
732–981–0090

400 DINER
400 N. Broad St., Elizabeth
908–354–9449

FOUR SEASONS DINER
3402 Rte. 9 South, Rio Grande
609–889–1666

FOUR STAR DINER
543 32nd St., Union City
201–866–0101

FRANKLIN DINER
Rte. 23, Franklin (Sussex County)
973–827–5588

FRANK'S DINER
51 Parsippany Rd., Whippany
973–428–9752

FRED'S BEACH HAVEN DINER
4th Street, Beach Haven
609–492–4269

FREEWAY DINER
Rte. 41, Deptford
856–227–6771

GALAXY DINER
293 St. Georges Ave., Rahway
732–388–4220

GALLERY DINER RESTAURANT
825 N. Pearl St., Bridgeton
856–455–1010

GALLOWAY DINER
245 W. White Horse Pike, Galloway
609–748–0033

GARDEN STATE DINER
Rte. 46 East, Dover

GARDEN STATE DINER
Terminal C, Newark-Liberty International
Airport
973–648–6791

GARDEN STATE DINER-RESTAURANT
Rte. 545 at Rte. 547, Wrightstown
856–723–5625

GATEWAY DINER
106 Broadway, Westville
856–456–5554

GERVASIO'S
14th and Boulevard, Surf City
609–494–7040

GK DINER
W. 21st St., Linden

GLAMIGO'S TEXAS WEINER/BBQ
551 Chancellor Ave., Irvington
973–371–7313

GLENWOOD DINER
265 Glenwood Ave., Bloomfield
973–748–1877

GOLDEN BELL DINER
3320 Rte. 9 South, Freehold
732–462–7259

GOLDEN CORNER
313 W. Union Ave., Bound Brook
732–469–3350

GOLDEN DAWN DINER
4387 Rte. 130 South, Edgewater Park
856–877–2236

GOLDEN DAWN DINER II
2090 White Horse–Mercerville Rd., Mercerville
609–890–2606

GOLDEN EAGLE DINER
Rte. 73, Maple Shade
856–235–8550

GOLDEN EAGLE DINER
239 Broad Ave., Palisades Park
201–947–3705

GOLDEN GATE DINER
2201 Nottingham Way, Hamilton
609–587–9800

GOLDEN HARVEST
591 Bloomfield Ave., Bloomfield
973–429–0124

GOLDEN PALACE DINER
2623 S. Delsea Dr. (Rte. 47), Vineland
856–692–5424

GOLDEN PALACE II DINER RESTAURANT
200 N. Virginia Ave., Penns Grove
856–299–3242

GOLDEN STAR RESTAURANT
Rte. 35 and Steiner Ave., Neptune City
732–988–6655

GOLDEN TOUCH DINER & RESTAURANT
Rte. 10, East Hanover
973–887–4193

GOODMAN'S DINER
180 Elmora Ave., Elizabeth
908–354–1802

GORGE'S DINER
774 Convery Blvd., Perth Amboy
732–324–8115

GOTHAM CITY DINER
550 Bergen Blvd., Ridgefield
201–943–5664

GREEK DELIGHTS
14 Park St., Montclair
973–783–9100

GUREK'S DINER
1469 Springfield Ave., Maplewood
973–761–9872

GUS'S DINER
135 Rte. 33 East, Manalapan
732–294–0006

HAGLER'S DINER
279 Kinderkamack Rd., Oradell
201–261–9719

HAMILTON DINER
1781 E. State St., Hamilton
609–587–2300

HAMPTON DINER
Rte. 206 North, Newton
973–383–1550

HARBOR RESTAURANT & DINER
613 White Horse Pike, Egg Harbor
609–965–0797

HARLEY DAWN DINER
1402 Black Horse Pike, Folsom
609–567–6084

HARRIS DINER
N. Park and Washington sts., East Orange
973–675–9703

HARRISON HOUSE DINER
Rtes. 45 and 322, Mullica Hill
856–478–6077

HARVEST ALL-AMERICAN DINER
2602 Rte. 130, Cinnaminson
856–829–4499

HATHAWAY'S DINER & RESTAURANT
Rte. 130 North, Cinnaminson
856–751–7319

HIBERNIA DINER RESTAURANT
9 Green Pond Rd., Rockaway
973–625–3255

HIGHTSTOWN DINER
151 Mercer St., Hightstown
609–443–4600

HILLARY DINER
1002 Harrison Ave., Harrison
201–955–0707

HILLSBOROUGH STAR DINER
842 Rte. 206, Hillsborough
908–281–9696

HILLSIDE RESTAURANT & DINER
Rte. 202 North, Oakland
201–337–1262

HOGAN'S RESTAURANT DINER
20 Central Ave., Midland Park
201–445–2849

HOLIDAY CITY DINER
600 Mule Rd., Toms River
732–244–4778

HOLLY BROOK DINER
1655 Rte. 38, Mount Holly
609–267–7699

HORIZON DINER
32 E. Bay Ave., Manahawkin
609–597–4771

HORIZON DINER
726 Rte. 17 North, Ramsey
201–825–1774

HORSESHOE DINER
Boyle Plaza, Jersey City

HOT SPOT DINER
17 Ave. A, Newark
973–242–3004

HUCK FINN DINER
2431 Morris Ave., Union
908–810–9000

INTERNATIONAL CUISINE DINER
428 Elizabeth Ave., Elizabeth
908–351–0704

ISLA BONITA GRILL
567 Valley Rd., West Orange
973–736–4410

ISLAND DINER
3212 Bayshore Ave., Brigantine
609–266–8773

JACKSON HOLE DINER
362 Grand Ave., Englewood
201–871–7444

JB'S DINER
205 Monmouth Rd., Freehold
732–866–0220

JEFFERSON DINER
Rte. 15, Jefferson
973–663–0233

JERSEY DINER
79 Rte. 202 North, Raritan Borough
908–7807–1222

JERSEY DINER RESTAURANT
328 S. White Horse Pike, Berlin
856–719–9339

JIMMY'S BROADWAY DINER
126 N. Broadway, South Amboy
732–721–9608

JM DINER
664 Bloomfield Ave., Glen Ridge

JOE'S DINER
Rte. 542, Wading River
609–812–1849

JOHN & ELAINE'S RESTAURANT
1103 Richmond Ave., Point Pleasant Beach
732–899–0089

JOHNNY B'S DINER
Rtes. 537 and 524, Freehold
732–409–6478

JOHNNY'S RESTAURANT
99 Water St., South River
732–238–1660

JOSE'S DINER
4 Hamburg Ave., Sussex Borough
973–702–2080

JT'S DINER
Rte. 173, Clinton
908–735–4212

JUBILEE PARK DINER
913 Allwood Rd., Clifton
973–773–6145

KENILWORTH DINER-RESTAURANT
614 Boulevard, Kenilworth
908–245–6565

KENNEDY FRIED CHICKEN
Haledon Ave. and Main St., Paterson

KENVIL DINER
405 Rte. 46, Kenvil
973–584–5599

KEY CITY DINER
Rte. 22, Lopatcong
908–859–9830

KING GEORGE DINER & RESTAURANT
721 Paterson-Hamburg Turnpike, Wayne
973–696–3010

KINGS BRIDGE DINER
44 Franklin Turnpike, Mahwah
201–529–9999

KLESS DINER
1212 Springfield Ave., Irvington
973–372–8672

KORYEOJOUNG
1645 Lemoine Ave., Fort Lee
201–585–0200

LACEY DINER
530 Lacey Rd., Forked River
609–693–5565

LAKEHURST DINER RESTAURANT
Rtes. 70 and 547, Manchester
732–657–9747

LA MIRAGE DINER
Rte. 9, Freehold
732–625–0330

LAMP POST DINER
6 Weeks Ave., North Wildwood
609–522–9348

LAND & SEA RESTAURANT DINER
20–12 Fairlawn Ave., Fair Lawn
201–794–7240

LARRY'S MARCO LITTLE DINER
905 Frank Rodgers Blvd., Harrison
973–481–1122

LEXINGTON DINER
351 Lexington Ave., Clifton
973–478–2900

LIBERTY DINER
501 S. Delsea Dr., Clayton
856–881–9413

LIBERTY DINER
2320 Rte. 130 North, North Brunswick
732–422–1898

LIBERTY TWO DINER
5254 Rte. 130 North, Mansfield
609–298–8933

LIGHTHOUSE DINER & RESTAURANT
1848 Hooper Ave., Toms River
732–255–8330

LINCOLN PARK DINER
11 Lincoln Park Plaza, Lincoln Park
973–694–9571

LINDA'S DINER & RESTAURANT
98 Main St., East Brunswick
732–251–6929

LINDEN HOUSE DINER
200 St. Georges Ave., Linden
908–486–3930

LISBOA BBQ
1 Lakeview Pl., Verona
973–571–9339

LITTLE FALLS DINER
9 Paterson Ave., Little Falls

LIVINGSTON DINER
360 E. Northfield Rd., Livingston
973–992–6339

LOS TRES HERMANOS
8 Railroad Ave., Hammonton
609–704–8244

LOUISE'S DINER
Rte. 173, Clinton

LOUKAS LAST AMERICAN DINER
3205 Rte. 22, Branchburg
908–253–6700

LUNA ROSA DINER
680 Martin Luther King Jr. Way, Paterson
201–977–8062

LYNDHURST DINER & RESTAURANT
540 Riverside Ave., Lyndhurst
201–933–7660

M
45 New St., Irvington
973–374–0400

MACK DINER
150 French St., New Brunswick

MAC'S DINER
1420 Rte. 23 North, Butler
973–283–9100

MAGNOLIA RESTAURANT & DINER
510 S. White Horse Pike, Magnolia
856–784–8424

MAIN & CLIFTON RESTAURANT DINER
341 Clifton Ave., Clifton
973–365–0333

MALAGA DINER
3433 Harding Hwy., Franklin Township
(Gloucester County)
856–694–5640

MALIBU DINER RESTAURANT
259 14th St., Hoboken
201–656–1595

MANALAPAN DINER & RESTAURANT
48 Rte. 9, Manalapan
732–462–7165

MANETA'S DINER
2654 S. Broad St., Trenton
609–888–0208

MANVILLE DINER
50 S. Main St., Manville
908–685–0930

MAPLE HILL DINER RESTAURANT
701 E. Main St., Maple Shade
856–779–1610

MAPLE LEAF DINER
165 Maplewood Ave., Maplewood
973–763–8833

MAPLEWOOD DINER
1473 Springfield Ave., Maplewood
973–763–6511

MARGE'S DINER
Rte. 9 at Rte. 83, Clermont
609–624–1798

MARINA DINER
Rte. 36 West, Belford
732–495–9749

MARKET TOWER
Market and Fleming sts., Newark

MARK TWAIN DINER RESTAURANT
1601 Morris Ave., Union
908–687–1680

MARLBORO RENAISSANCE DINER
143 Rte. 9, Marlboro
732–972–8087

MARLTON DINER
781 Rte. 70 West, Evesham
856–797–8858

MARYA DINER
309 Main St., Sayreville
732–432–5890

MA'S MUNCHIES DINER
449 Ferry St., Newark
973–344–1140

MASTORIS DINER RESTAURANT
144 Rte. 130 South, Bordentown
609–298–4650

MATTHEWS COLONIAL DINER
4 Franklin Turnpike, Waldwick
201–447–1411

MATTHEWS DINER & PANCAKE HOUSE
430 S. Washington Ave., Bergenfield
201–385–9496

MAX'S BAGEL & GRILL
361 Newark Ave., Jersey City

MAYS LANDING DINER
6177 Harding Hwy. (Rte. 40), Mays Landing
609–625–5051

MEADOWLANDS DINER
320 Rte. 17, Carlstadt
201–935–5444

MEADOWS DINER
101 S. Black Horse Pike, Blackwood
856–232–9099

MED PORT DINER & RESTAURANT
122 Rte. 70 East, Medford
856–654–4001

MEL'S DINER
5015 Rte. 34, Howell
732–919–1500

MEMORY LANE DINER
1137 Fischer Blvd., Toms River
732–270–1355

MENLO PARK DINER
Rte. 1 South, Edison
732–494–1760

METRO CAFE DINER
80 Rte. 202/31, Ringoes
908–284–2240

METRO VIEW DINER
468 Halendon Ave., Haledon
201–942–5151

MICHAEL'S RESTAURANT
2991 Rte. 1 South, Lawrenceville
609–530–1676

MIDDLETOWN DINER
1887 Rte. 35, Middletown
732–671–1316

MIDLAND DINER
1002 Harrison Ave., Kearny
201–246–1123

MIDTOWN GRILL
1218 Main Ave., Clifton
973–546–0121

MILLBURN DINER
72 Essex St., Millburn
973–376–0504

MILLVILLE QUEEN DINER
109 E. Broad St., Millville
856–327–0900

MINI-MAC RESTAURANT & DINER
209 Rte. 206 South, Chester
908–879–9813

MISS AMERICA DINER
322 West Side Ave., Jersey City
201–333–5468

MOM'S DINER
Rte. 1 North, Avenel

MOM'S DINER
Rte. 33, East Windsor
609–448–8544

MOM'S PANCAKE HOUSE
Tonnele Ave. (Rte. 1) and 78th St., North Bergen

MONTVILLE DINER
Rte. 46, Pine Brook
973–575–0326

MORRISTOWN DINER
73 Morris Ave., Morristown
973–538–0228

MOUNTAINSIDE RESTAURANT DINER
198 Rte. 206, Byram
973–347–8787

MOUNTAIN VIEW DINER & RESTAURANT
1203 Bound Brook Rd., Middlesex
732–469–5414

MOUSTACHE BILL'S DINER
8th and Broadway, Barnegat Light
609–494–0155

MRS. G'S
Rte. 1 North, Lawrenceville

NAUTILIS DINER
97 Main St., Madison
973–377–8484

NEIGHBOR DINER
1012 Mt. Tabor Rd., Morris Plains
973–285–1155

NEVADA DINER RESTAURANT
293 Broad St., Bloomfield
973–743–9393

NEW ANDERSON DINER
703 Anderson Ave., Cliffside Park
201–941–4808

NEW ATCO DINER
348 White Horse Pike, Atco
856–767–5958

NEW BLACK HORSE DINER &
RESTAURANT
152 N. Black Horse Pike, Mount Ephraim
856–742–8989

NEW GEET'S DINER
Black Horse Pike and Sicklerville Rd.,
Williamstown
856–629–7433

NEW GOLDEN DAWN DINER
Rtes. 73 and 38, Maple Shade
856–234–8654

NEW HERITAGE DINER
80 River St., Hackensack
201–342–6757

NEW SPARTA DINER
80 Woodport Rd., Sparta
973–729–2425

NEW STAR DINER
380 Rte. 46, South Hackensack
201–440–3704

NEWTON DINER
931 White Horse Pike, Haddon
856–854–9100

NICHOLAS DINER
88 E. Railway Ave., Paterson
973–278–2556

NICK'S HOMETOWN DINER
2929 Rte. 130 South, Delran
856–461–2419

NORTH STAR 23 DINER
1420 Rte. 23, Wayne
973–709–1166

NORTHVALE DINER
247 Livingston Ave., Northvale
201–767–6267

NUBIAN FLAVOR
410 Springfield Ave., Newark
973–242–2238

NUTLEY DINER
372 Centre St., Nutley
973–235–0937

OASIS DINER
9 Marshall Hill Rd., West Milford
973–728–8941

OASIS DINER & RESTAURANT
683 Main Ave., Passaic
973–773–7474

OCEAN BAY DINER
1517 Ocean Ave., Point Pleasant Beach
732–295–1070

OCEAN QUEEN DINER
906 Rte. 70, Brick
732–458–7022

OLD BRIDGE DINER FAMILY RESTAURANT
1146 Englishtown Rd., Old Bridge
732–251–4144

OLD TOWNE DINER
2050 Rte. 50, Upper Township
609–628–4688

OLGA'S DINER
Rtes. 70 and 73, Marlton
856–596–1700

OLYMPIA DINER
460 Maple Ave., Elizabeth
908–289–2465

OLYMPIC DINER
Rte. 40 at Rte. 9, Pleasantville

OMEGA DINER & CAFE
1337 Rte. 1, North Brunswick
732–745–2628

1–9 CHINESE RESTAURANT
Rte. 1 South, Avenel
732–602–8863

ORIGINAL GOLDEN PIGEON
39 Landis Ave., Bridgeton
856–451–0940

PALACE DINER
363 George St., New Brunswick
732–545–8116

PALACE DINER RESTAURANT
Rte. 73, Berlin
856–767–5061

PAPPY'S DINER
315 Union Blvd., Totowa
973–595–1701

PARAMOUNT DINER
1803 Rte. 35 South, Sayreville
732–316–9600

PARK PLACE DINER
1040 Rte. 34, Matawan
732–290–1978

PARK RIDGE DINER
125 Kinderkamack Rd., Park Ridge
201–391–4242

PARKSIDE DINER
1769 Parkside Ave., Ewing
609–883–2123

PARKWAY DINER
Rte. 46, Elmwood Park
201–791–5342

PARK WEST DINER
Rte. 46 West, Little Falls
973–256–2767

PARK WOOD DINER
1958 Springfield Ave., Maplewood
973–313–3990

PARTVIEW DINER
354 Fairview Ave., Fairview
201–945–4102

PAT'S ORIGINAL DINER
1300 Broad St., Trenton
609–392–2024

PAUL AND CHRISTA'S DINER & FAMILY
RESTAURANT
19 Rte. 181 South, Lake Hopatcong
973–663–4405

PAULA'S FAMILY RESTAURANT
Rte. 130 South, Cinnaminson
856–829–7350

PAUL'S FAMILY DINER
Rte. 46, Mountain Lakes
973–627–4436

PAUL'S OCEANSIDE DINER &
RESTAURANT
562 Rte. 9, Waretown
609–693–3296

PB'S DINER
Rte. 47 North, Glassboro
856–881–1579

PENN QUEEN DINER
7349 Rte. 130, Pennsauken
856–662–1928

PETER PANK DINER
Rte. 9 North, Sayreville
732–721–2850

PETER'S DINER
1741 S. Black Horse Pike, Monroe Township
856–740–4422

PHILLIPSBURG DINER
1102 Rte. 22, Lopatcong
908–213–9995

PHILY DINER
31 S. Black Horse Pike, Runnemede
856–939–4322

PHOENIX DINER
200 White Horse Pike, Absecon
609–646–1958

PILGRIM DINER-RESTAURANT
82 Pompton Ave., Cedar Grove
973–239–2900

PINE BROOK GRILL
466 Boonton Turnpike, Lincoln Park
973–305–9005

PINK CADILLAC DINER
3801 Atlantic Ave., Wildwood
609–522–8288

PLAZA DINER
126 Bloomfield Ave., Bloomfield
973–748–3646

PLAZA DINER
2066 Rte. 27, Edison
732–287–4455

PLAZA DINER
686 Rte. 70, Lakehurst
732–657–7771

PLAZA DINER
1262 Paterson Plank Rd., Secaucus
201–864–1531

PLAZA DINER RESTAURANT
2045 Lemoine Ave., Fort Lee
201–944–8681

PLAZA 46 DINER
380 Rte. 46, South Hackensack
201–440–3704

PLAZA 23 DINER
411 Rte. 23, Pompton Plains
973–835–1952

THE POINT
160 Bergen Blvd., Fairview
201–943–6719

POINT DINER
MacArthur Blvd. and Circle Dr., Somers Point
609–927–2284

POINT 40 DINER
Rtes. 40 and 77, Pole Tavern
856–358–2882

POMONA DINER
275 S. Pomona Rd., Pomona
609–804–0555

POMPTON LAKES DINER
246 Wanaque Ave., Pompton Lakes
973–248–1700

POMPTON QUEEN DINER & RESTAURANT
710 Rte. 23, Pompton Plains
973–835–2086

PONZIO'S BROOKLAWN
Rte. 130 North, Brooklawn
856–456–3690

PONZIO'S RESTAURANT
Rte. 70 East at Rte. 41, Cherry Hill
856–428–4808

PORTO VIA CAFFE & SPORTS BAR (MAX'S GRILL)
731 Harrison Ave., Harrison
973–483–2012

PREAKNESS RESTAURANT & DINER
1220 Hamburg Turnpike, Wayne
973–694–9260

PRESTIGE DINER
610 Rte. 33 East, East Windsor
609–443–1211

PRESTIGE DINER & RESTAURANT
1318 Springfield Ave., New Providence
908–665–0211

PRIMAVERA RESTAURANT DINER
Rte. 73, Cherry Hill
856–424–8585

PRINCE INN DINER
4520 Rte. 130 North, Burlington
856–386–5522

PRINCESS DINER
1809 Rte. 23, Wayne
973–628–7331

PRINCESS MARIA DINER
2044 Rte. 35, Wall
732–282–1722

PRINCETONIAN DINER
3509 Rte. 1, West Windsor
609–452–2272

QUINTON DINER & RESTAURANT
534 Quinton Rd., Quinton
856–935–8011

RACEWAY DINER
135 Rte. 36, West Long Branch
732–483–9080

RAILWAY DINER
197 E. Railway Ave., Paterson
973–523–3800

RAINBOW DINER
157 Fries Mill Rd., Turnersville
856–227–4174

RAINBOW DINER RESTAURANT
Rte. 70, Brick
732–840–1555

RANDOLPH DINER
517 Rte. 10, Randolph
973–328–2400

READINGTON DINER
452 Rte. 22 West, Whitehouse Station
908–534–6777

RED HAWK DINER
College Ave. and Webster Rd., Montclair State University, Little Falls
973–655–4057

RED LION TOWN & COUNTRY DINER
Rtes. 70 and 206, Southampton
856–859–2301

RED OAK DINER & BAKERY
1217 Rte. 206, Montgomery
609–430–8200

RED OAK DINER RESTAURANT
2191 Fletcher Ave., Fort Lee
201–461–8668

RED TOWER
500 Park Ave., Plainfield
908–561–0353

RED TOWER II
864 Rte. 22 East, North Plainfield
908–754–0002

REGENT DINER
6849 Rte. 9 North, Howell
732–364–9157

REGI'S DINER
1135 E. Jersey St., Elizabeth
908–527–7344

RENA'S DINER
1326 South Ave., Plainfield
908–756–7900

REO DINER & RESTAURANT
392 Amboy Ave., Woodbridge
732–634–9200

RIDGEDALE DINER RESTAURANT
474 Ridgedale Ave., East Hanover
973–428–0700

RIDGEFIELD PARK DINER
30 Mt. Vernon, Ridgefield Park
201–641–3250

RIO GRANDE DINER & FAMILY
RESTAURANT
1305 Rte. 47, Rio Grande
609–886–7376

RISING STAR DINER
1239 Roosevelt Ave., Carteret
732–969–0276

RITZ DINER
72 E. Mt. Pleasant Ave., Livingston
973–533–1213

RIVER EDGE DINER
516 Kinderkamack Rd., River Edge
201–262–4976

RIVERSIDE DINER
208 N. Main St., Lanoka Harbor
609–242–7580

RIVER STAR DINER
14 Rte. 57, Hackettstown
908–979–0626

RIVERVIEW DINER
7850 River Rd., North Bergen
201–868–5400

ROADSIDE DINER
Rtes. 33 and 34, Wall
732–919–1199

ROCHELLE PARK DINER CAFE
222 Rochelle Ave., Rochelle
201–843–0068

ROCKAWAY DINER
116 Rte. 46, Rockaway Borough
973–983–1350

RONEY'S
55 Haddon Ave., Haddon
856–854–9746

RONNIE'S CAFE DINER
664 Mantoloking Rd., Brick
732–920–2335

ROXBURY DINER
101 Rte. 10, Roxbury
973–584–2818

ROYAL CLIFFS RESTAURANT
717 Palisades Ave., Englewood Cliffs
201–569–7277

ROYAL DINER
Rte. 22 East, Branchburg

ROYAL DINER
150 Rte. 31 South, Washington
908–689–7486

RUSTIC MILL DINER
109 North Ave., Cranford
908–272–7016

SADDLE BROOK DINER
30 Market St., Saddle Brook
201–843–5929

SAGE DINER
1958 Springfield Ave., Maplewood
973–761–1632

SAGE DINER RESTAURANT
1170 Rte. 73, Mount Laurel
856–727–0770

SALEES DINER
334 Main St., Ogdensburg
973–209–2603

SALEM OAK DINER
113 W. Broadway, Salem
609–935–1305

SAND CASTLE DINER
634 Atlantic City Blvd., Beachwood
732–244–8881

SCHUYLER DINER
500 Schuyler Ave., Lyndhurst
201–933–6196

SCOTCHWOOD DINER-RESTAURANT
1934 Rte. 22, Scotch Plains
908–322–4114

SEAPORT DINER
798 Dowd Ave., Elizabeth
908–351–4510

SEAPORT DINER
83 Broad St., Keyport
732–264–9659

SECAUCUS METRO DINER
130 County Ave., Secaucus
201–974–1551

SERVICE DINER
935 River Rd., Garfield
973–772–2033

SEVENTEENTH STREET DINER
1634 Park Ave., Weehawkin
201–863–9230

SEVILLE DINER
Rte. 18 and Hillsdale Rd., East Brunswick
732–254–1125

SEVILLE DINER RESTAURANT
289 Broadway, Westwood
201–664–8696

SHALIMAR RESTAURANT
1335 Oak Tree Rd., Iselin
732–283–3350

SHAMONG DINER
7 Willow Grove Rd., Shamong
609–268–1182

SHANIA'S DINER
25 Madison Ave., Mount Holly
609–518–1952

SHERBAN'S DINER
Front St., South Plainfield
908–755–7427

SHORE DINER
6710 Tilton Rd., Pleasantville
609–641–3669

SHORT STOP DINER (DUNKIN DONUTS)
315 Franklin St., Bloomfield

SILVER COIN DINER
Rte. 206 and White Horse Pike, Hammonton
609–561–6974

SILVER DINER
2131 Rte. 38, Cherry Hill
856–910–1240

SILVERTON DINER
1848 Hooper Ave., Toms River
732–255–3368

SIX BROTHERS DINER
Rte. 46, Little Falls
973–256–2510

SKYLARK DINER
Rte. 1 North, Edison

SKYLINE RESTAURANT & DINER
16 Greenwood Lake Turnpike, Ringwood
973–831–5777

SKYWAY DINER
Central Ave. and 2nd St., Kearny
973–589–6823

SOMERSET DINER
1040 Easton Ave., Somerset
732–828–5424

SPINNING WHEEL DINER
Rte. 22 East, Lebanon
908–534–2577

SPOTSWOOD FAMILY DINER
RESTAURANT
12 Snowhill St., Spotswood
732–416–1930

SPRINGFIELD DINER
234 Morris Ave., Springfield
973–564–8001

STAFFORD DINER
1388 Rte. 72, Manahawkin
609–978–1948

STAR DINER & CAFE
325 W. Spruce Ave., North Wildwood
609–729–4900

STARDUST DINER
28 Rte. 46, Hackettstown
908–979–0300

STARVIEW DINER
491 Williamstown–New Freedom Rd.,
Sicklerville
856–728–2880

STARVIEW DINER
9 White Horse Pike, Somerdale
856–784–4224

STATE LINE DINER
375 Rte. 17 South, Mahwah
201–529–3353

STATE STREET DINER
728 State St., Perth Amboy
732–442–9433

STEPHANIE'S DINER & BBQ
8 Centre St. Nutley
973–661–4441

STIRLING HOUSE DINER SEAFOOD
PAVILION
1079 Valley Rd., Stirling
908–647–7105

STRATFORD DINER
19 S. White Horse Pike, Stratford
856–435–4300

SUBURBAN DINER
172 Rte. 17 North, Paramus
201–261–2605

SUMMIT DINER
Summit Ave. and Union Pl., Summit
908–277–3256

SUNLIGHT DINER
590 Belleville Turnpike, Kearny
201–997–9510

SUNRISE DINER
479 Rte. 17 North, Paramus
201–967–0190

SUNRISE DINER
61 W. Westfield Ave., Roselle
908–241–1335

SUNSET DINER
335 Rte. 22 East, Green Brook
732–356–2674

SUNSET DINER
3315 Sunset Ave., Ocean
732–775–0080

SUPERIOR DINER
464 Smith St., Perth Amboy
732–442–3772

SURFSIDE WEST DINER
3 Cresse St., Middle Township
609–522–2439

SUSSEX QUEEN DINER
289 Rte. 23, Sussex
973–702–7321

TENAFLY DINER
16 W. Railroad Ave., Tenafly
201–567–5522

THAILAND
291 Central Ave., Clark
732–388–4441

32ND STREET DINER
698 Broadway, Bayonne
201–437–9100

THORPE'S DINER
602 Communipaw Ave., Jersey City
201–324–1441

THREE FLAGS DINER
332 Atlantic City Blvd., Toms River
732–349–3336

THREE GEE'S DINER
305 N. Mill Rd., Vineland
856–690–9135

TICK-TOCK DINER
Rte. 3, Clifton
973–777–0511

TICO'S EN MEXICO RESTAURANT
221 Main St., Chatham
973–635–5040

TIFFANY DINER-RESTAURANT
1045 Rte. 17 South, Ramsey
201–825–3572

TIME TO EAT DINER
Rte. 206, Somerville Circle, Bridgewater
908–704–9221

TOMMY'S DINER
235 Paterson Ave., Wallington
973–773–6180

TOM SAWYER RESTAURANT
98 Ridgewood Ave., Paramus
201–262–0111

TOM'S DINER
1200 Rte. 46, Roxbury
973–584–8667

TOMS RIVER DINER
Rte. 37, Toms River
732–929–0440

TONY'S FREEHOLD GRILLE
59 E. Main St., Freehold
732–431–8607

TOPS DINER
500 Passaic Ave., East Newark
973–481–0490

TOWN & COUNTRY DINER
Rte. 130 North, Bordentown
609–298–1685

TOWN & COUNTRY RESTAURANT
Rte. 37 West, Toms River
732–341–0822

TOWNSQUARE DINER
320 Rte. 15, Wharton
973–366–7244

TRAIN DINER RESTAURANT
548 Passaic, West Caldwell
973–227–5694

TRAVELERS DINER
Rte. 46 East, Dover
973–361–7003

TRIANGLE DINER
112 Goffle Rd., Hawthorne
973–427–8408

TRI-BORO DINER
515 Essex St., Hackensack
201–343–7651

TROPICANA DINER
545 Morris Ave., Elizabeth
908–351–7775

TRUCK STOP DINER
Hackensack Ave., Kearny
973–344–4098

TUNNEL DINER
184 14th St., Jersey City
201–653–4523

UNCLE BUCK'S DINER
2 Market St., Belvidere
908–475–3668

UNION PLAZA DINER
Rte. 22, Union
908–686–4403

UNIVERSITY DINER
580 North Ave., Union
908–354–3110

USA DINER
1277 Rte. 23, Butler
973–283–2283

USA DINER
431 Rte. 130, Windsor
609–448–1322

US 1 DINER
Rte. 1 South and Industrial La., Linden
908–862–0245

VALLEY DINER
267 Closter Dock Rd., Closter
201–767–7530

VEGAS DINER
14th and New Jersey aves., North Wildwood
609–729–5511

VERONA DINER
676 Bloomfield Ave., Verona
973–239–3560

VERONICA PLAZA DINER & RESTAURANT
84 Veronica Ave., Somerset
732–214–0880

VERSAILLES DINER
516 Rte. 46 East, Fairfield
973–227–0508

VICKI'S DINER
110 E. Broad St., Westfield
908–233–6887

VICTORY DINER RESTAURANT
181 Rte. 37 East, Toms River
732–286–1190

VILLA NOVA DINER
8601 Atlantic Ave., Wildwood
609–522–2235

VINCENTOWN DINER
Rtes. 38 and 206, Vincentown
856–267–3033

VIP DINER
175 Sip Ave., Jersey City
201–792–1400

WASHINGTON DINER RESTAURANT
Rte. 31 North, Washington
908–689–3059

WAYNE HILLS DINER
1465 Hamburg Turnpike, Wayne
973–628–1824

WEBER'S COLONIAL DINER
136 White Horse Pike, Audubon
856–546–5296

WESTAMPTON FAMILY DINER
1857 Rte. 541, Westampton
856–265–7065

WESTFIELD DINER
309 North Ave., Westfield
908–233–5200

WEST MILFORD DINER & FAMILY
RESTAURANT
2020 Greenwood Lake Turnpike, Hewitt
973–728–1010

WESTMONT DINER
317 Haddon Ave., Haddon
856–854–7220

WEST ORANGE DINER
270 Main St., West Orange
973–736–8333

WEST SIDE DINER
324 Rte. 46 West, Denville
973–983–1818

WESTWOOD DINER
201 Old Hook Rd., Westwood
201–664–7455

WHIPPANY DINER
417 Rte. 10, Whippany
973–428–5054

WHITE CIRCLE SYSTEM
176 Bloomfield Ave., Bloomfield
973–429–1965

WHITE DIAMOND
1208½ E. Grand St., Elizabeth
908–352–8555

WHITE DIAMOND
Raritan Rd. and Central Ave., Clark
732–574–8053

WHITE DIAMOND
510 E. St. Georges Ave., Linden
908–486–1707

WHITE HORSE DINER
50 S. White Horse Pike, Berlin
856–753–8863

WHITE HOUSE FAMILY RESTAURANT
Rte. 46 East, Little Falls
973–256–6650

WHITE MANA
470 Tonnele Ave. (Rte. 1), Jersey City
201–963–1441

WHITE MANNA
358 River St., Hackensack
201–342–0914

WHITE ROSE SYSTEM
154 Woodbridge Ave., Highland Park
732–572–9829

WHITE ROSE SYSTEM
1301 Elizabeth Ave., Linden
908–486–9651

WHITE ROSE SYSTEM
201 1st Ave., Roselle
908–241–9639

WHITE STAR DINER
715 Front St., Plainfield
908–756–5411

WHITE STAR RESTAURANT
100 Maple Ave., South Plainfield
908–561–0850

WHITMAN DINER
Rte. 42 North, Turnersville
856–228–4449

WILDWOOD DINER
4005 Atlantic Ave., Wildwood
609–522–8000

WILLIE'S DINER
9 State St., Bloomfield
973–748–7414

WINDSOR DINER
1030 Raritan Rd., Clark
732–382–7755

WINDSOR DINER
298 Ferry St., Newark
973–622–9093

WINSLOW FAMILY DINER & RESTAURANT
491 Williamstown Rd., Winslow
856–875–4700

WISDOM DINER
1024 Rte. 206, Bordentown
609–298–3205

WOODSTOWN DINER RESTAURANT &
LOUNGE
16 East Ave., Woodstown
856–769–1140

YANKEE TOWER DINER
174 Broad Ave., Fairview
201–943–4608

YELLOW ROSE DINER
41 Rte. 36, Hazlet
732–739–8811

YETTER'S DINER
Rte. 206 North, Augusta
973–383–5641

ZIKOS DINER
610 Delilah Rd., Pleasantville
609–646–6551

The Olympia Diner, formerly on Route 40 in Carneys Point, now in Jessup, Maryland.

ACKNOWLEDGMENTS

My thanks, first of all, to all the diner owners who took time from their ever-busy schedules to sit down and talk to me, a complete stranger, about their diners, their business, and their lives.

And to the waitresses, cooks, customers, and enthusiasts who told me why they wouldn't work, or eat, or hang out anywhere but a diner.

Several people got me off to a good start with their advice and counsel: Tim Ferrante, Ken Parker, Christine Guedon-DeConcini, and Steve Lintner.

Many thanks to Mary Mastoris for the invaluable old photos of the Burlington and Hightstown diners; to Harold Kullman at Kullman Industries; Phil DeRaffele at DeRaffele Manufacturing Co.; Ralph Musi at Sunrise Diner Manufacturers Inc.; Pat Fodero, formerly of Fodero Dining Car Co.; and Herb Enyart at Paramount Modular Concepts for their accounts of their respective companies' histories, and an extra thanks to Pat, for the packet of photos and documents, and Herb, for the great old photos off his wall.

Thanks to Randy Garbin, publisher of *Roadside,* the bible of the diner industry, and Susan Germain.

And Paul Hirshorn and Steve Izenour, for the evocative White Tower pictures; Babe Weed, for the wonderful photos and menus from the Club Diner; Barb and Bob McAllister, for the vintage photos and menus from the Salem Oak and the Elite diners; John Stavros, who took the framed picture of the original Olga's Diner off the wall and let me copy it; Momir Saranovic at the Dumont Crystal, for the video; Adele Yuknus

Sugar for take-out coffee, Summit Diner.

Teamster's Diner, Fairfield.

Olesen, for calling me up and telling me the story of Tony's Lunch; and to George Forakis at the Reo Diner, for the VE Day photo.

Special thanks to John Baeder, for the loan of his paintings; also to Steve Boksenbaum, for the loan of his work.

To Kathie and everyone at Freese Camera in New Brunswick: thanks for making me look good.

Colleagues at work offered support and encouragement, especially Sue Livio and Rose Szakacs; Winnie Zagariello and Betty Selingo, the best librarians in New Jersey; and Charles Johnson, who more than anyone else kept me in the journalism business—and on my toes.

I can't forget my mom, Connie Genovese, my Trenton diner scout and "agent."

Nor can I forget Marilyn Campbell at Rutgers University Press, for her wisdom and expert advice on this book and *Roadside New Jersey;* Marlie Wasserman, director of Rutgers University Press (welcome back!); Sue Llewellyn, my copyeditor; and Tricia Politi, production coordinator, and John Romer, designer, for making this book beautiful.

And, finally, to Marvin Krupnick, who not only let me flip through his amazing diner postcard collection but made copies from the cards I had selected for this book and drove all the way from his Pennsylvania home to East Brunswick to drop them off.

MANASQUAN, NEW JERSEY
May 1996

ABOUT THE AUTHOR

PETER GENOVESE, a feature writer for *The Star-Ledger*, eats, lives—even dreams—New Jersey. The author of *Roadside New Jersey, The Great American Roadtrip,* and *The Jersey Shore Uncovered* (all published by Rutgers University Press), he has driven more than one million miles around the state in the past thirty years.

Liberty Diner, North Brunswick. Photo by Joe McLaughlin.